D0361544

FORBIDDEN KNOWLEDGE:

SEX

101 Sensual Acts NOT Everyone Should Know How to Do

adams
media

Published by Adams Media, an F+W Publications Company
57 Littlefield Street
Avon, MA 02322
www.adamsmedia.com

ISBN 10: 1-60550-033-X
ISBN 13: 978-1-60550-033-1

Printed in the United States of America

This publication is designed to provide accurate and authoritative information
with regard to the subject matter covered. It is sold with the understanding
that the publisher is not engaged in rendering legal, accounting, or other
professional advice. If legal advice or other expert assistance is required,
the services of a competent professional person should be sought.
—From a Declaration of Principles jointly adopted by a Committee of the
American Bar Association and a Committee of Publishers and Associations

Many of the designations used by manufacturers and sellers to distinguish
their product are claimed as trademarks. Where those designations appear in
this book and Adams Media was aware of a trademark claim, the designations
have been printed with initial capital letters.

Photographs Istockphoto.com
Illustrations by Clodhopper Design and Istockphoto.com
Design by Clodhopper Design

This book is available at quantity discounts for bulk purchases.
For information, please call 1-800-289-0963.

FORBIDDEN KNOWLEDGE:

SEX

101 Sensual Acts **NOT** Everyone Should Know How to Do

INTRODUCTION:

Welcome to the book that won't tell you how to have sex. Why not? Because you already know how. We promise not to tell you how to get into the missionary position. We promise not to tell you how to light an aromatherapy candle and gaze into each other's eyes. And we definitely won't tell you how to practice romantic foreplay or put a condom on.

Since you already know how to put tab A into slot B and press button C, our proud aim is to furnish you with a whole load of filthy information you probably DON'T know. We promise to go where other sex books dare not. Virgins and prudes: step away now—close the cover of this bad, BAD book, breathe deeply and go and look at something on cookery or horticulture.

The rest of you can read on, basking in the knowledge that by the end of this book you'll know how to recognize an asphyxiophiliac, have a successful threesome, write your own erotica, have an affair, perform auto-fellatio, and master female ejaculation. You'll also know all sorts of kinky stuff about domination, submission, ropes, and anal sex. Plus you'll have eight different ways to tell someone they're crap in bed, and 50 different ways to invite someone into the sack.

NOTICE: TO ALL CONCERNED

005679821

Keep common sense in mind as you read this book—imagine your parents standing behind you shaking their heads disapprovingly if you find yourself tempted to do something you'll regret. For example, it's one thing to KNOW how to make your own contraception, and another thing to actually DO it. The same goes for pretending to be a virgin. Because we wish you a safe and pleasant sexual journey, please keep sex consensual, respectful, healthy, and safe at all times. Sex is great—but not when it gives you a STD, an unwanted pregnancy, or makes you feel miserable. If in any doubt, use the information in this book for showing off at dinner parties rather than for practicing with a partner. And, as your mom would tell you, if you wouldn't put something in your mouth, don't stick it in any other orifice. Apart from that—enjoy!

CONTENTS

1. Have Webcam Sex —————————————————————— 8
2. Make a Woman Ejaculate ———————————————— 10
3. Be a Good Dom ——————————————————————— 13
4. Find His P-Spot ——————————————————————— 16
5. Become a Sex Therapist ———————————————— 20
6. Perform Auto-Fellatio —————————————————— 23
7. Behave like an Eighteenth Century Rake ——— 25
8. Have Remote Control Sex ——————————————— 27
9. Get a Sex Change ——————————————————— 29
10. Make Fake Jism ——————————————————————— 32
11. Write Erotica ——————————————————————— 35
12. Make a Backdoor Entrance ——————————————— 37
13. Deal with an Obscene Phone Call —————————— 41
14. Ejaculate Internally ——————————————————— 43
15. Have Gourmet Sex ——————————————————— 45
16. Compile a Sex Library ————————————————— 47
17. Practice *Kama Sutra* —————————————————— 49
18. Tell if She's Had an Orgasm ——————————————— 51
19. Have Coitus à Mammilia ———————————————— 53
20. Have an Affair ——————————————————————— 55
21. Have Sex in Water ——————————————————— 58
22. Cure Impotence ——————————————————————— 60
23. Have Sex in an Elevator ———————————————— 63
24. Shoot Your Own Porn ————————————————— 65
25. Delay Ejaculation for an Hour ————————————— 67
26. Make Your Own Sex Toys ——————————————— 70
27. Cast a Sex Spell ——————————————————————— 72
28. Tell Someone They're Crap in Bed ————————— 74
29. Have Sex with the Same Person for the Rest of Your Life ——— 77
30. Spot The 8 Main Sexual Styles of Men ————————— 80
31. Spot The 8 Main Sexual Styles of Women ————— 83
32. Do a Vaginal Workout ————————————————— 85
33. Make Your Penis Bigger ————————————————— 87
34. Join the Mile High Club ———————————————— 91
35. Back Out of an Orgy —————————————————— 93
36. Recognize a Sex Addict ————————————————— 97
37. Become an Erotic Film Buff ——————————————— 99
38. Decipher Sexual Slang ————————————————— 101
39. Tell if Someone Wants to Have Sex with You ——— 103
40. Make All-Natural Contraceptives ———————————— 106
41. Make a Love Potion —————————————————— 109
42. Boost Sperm Count ——————————————————— 113
43. Play the Dice Game in Bed ——————————————— 115
44. Use an Egg as a Sexual Object —————————————— 117
45. Have a Successful Threesome ——————————————— 119
46. Have Mythical Sex ——————————————————— 123
47. Have Satanic Sex ——————————————————————— 125
48. Pretend to Be a Virgin ————————————————— 129
49. Get in Someone's Pants by Pretending to Be Gay — 132
50. Get into Someone's Pants by Pretending to Be Frigid — 134
51. Make Men Think You like Small Penises ————————— 136

52. Make Women Think You've Got a Huge Penis ——— 138
53. Make Traditional Aphrodisiacs ——— 140
54. Make Spanish Fly ——— 142
55. Ask for Sex 50 Different Ways ——— 144
56. Throw a Sex Party ——— 146
57. Do Clittage ——— 148
58. Have a Tantric Orgasm ——— 150
59. Leave Gracefully After a One-Night Stand ——— 152
60. Become a Sex Surrogate ——— 157
61. Handle a Foot Fetish ——— 160
62. Furnish a Sex Chamber ——— 162
63. Sculpt Your Pubic Hair ——— 164
64. Do 23 Positions During a One-Night Stand ——— 166
65. Find Her A-Spot ——— 170
66. Fist for the First Time ——— 173
67. Cure Priapism ——— 175
68. Realize You're a Porn Addict ——— 177
69. Seduce Someone on the Phone ——— 179
70. Be a Good Sub ——— 182
71. Do Analingus ——— 184
72. Look Cool While Stripping—for Guys ——— 187
73. Do a Standing 69 ——— 190
74. Tie Someone Up During Sex ——— 192
75. Give a Kinky Blowjob ——— 194
76. Play "Seduce the Bottle" ——— 196
77. Indulge a Pygophiliac ——— 198
78. Be an Ethical Slut ——— 200
79. Deep Throat ——— 202
80. Spot "The Clap" ——— 204
81. Advertise for Sex ——— 206
82. Give Earth-Shattering Cunnilingus ——— 209
83. Have Sex in Crowded Places ——— 211
84. Find Your Inner Sexual Animal ——— 213
85. Live Without Sex ——— 215
86. Lap Dance like a Professional ——— 217
87. Get in the Mood When You're Not in the Mood ——— 219
88. Eat Your Way to Stronger Orgasms ——— 221
89. Prepare for a Dirty Weekend ——— 223
90. Have Fantastic Sex Without a Partner ——— 225
91. Be a Candaulist ——— 228
92. Give the Perfect Kiss ——— 231
93. Use a Penis Pump ——— 233
94. Be Creative with a Rabbit ——— 236
95. Be a Sex Pest ——— 238
96. Tell Someone You've Got an STD ——— 240
97. Be a Sex Bore ——— 243
98. Make Pain Erotic ——— 246
99. Choose the Best Vibrator ——— 249
100. Use Anal Beads ——— 252
101. Recognize an Asphyxiophiliac ——— 254

1. Have Webcam Sex:

Having sex via a webcam is an essential 21st-century sex skill. Here are ten tips to make your show go off with a bang.

1) It's no use giving a porn-star performance if you haven't got all the techy stuff right first. Dim lighting, a slow internet connection, and a poorly positioned camera can mean your sex partner ends up yawning rather than coming. So do all the boring stuff…, then enjoy the naughty stuff.

2) Prepare. Prepare. Prepare. If you're going to use lube, vibrators, butt plugs, and other sex aids, keep them within spitting distance. And powered up and ready to go. Excusing yourself while you go and rummage for some fresh batteries isn't conducive to mind-blowing sex.

3) Take your webcam to the bedroom and "share" a glass of wine and a chat with your lover—hey, sex via the internet can be romantic too. Then as you undress, keep your whole body in view. Porn style close-ups can come later.

4) Once naked move your hands very slowly across your body—too fast and the movement will blur. Of course blurring can be exciting. It says "I'm too hot to pace myself"—but save that for your climax scene.

5) Stay in sync with your partner. Just like love in the real world, if he shoots his load while she's still getting her bra off, it's not going to work.

6) If your lover gets coy or inhibited, step in with a suggestion or a compliment. Or a downright command—if that's what you're into.

7) Don't forget the sound effects—you need to hear as well as see each other. Moan. Sigh. Verbalize.

8) When you're getting close to the grand finale, position yourself so that your lover can see a close-up of your face or genitals—or both if you can manage it.

9) Don't roll out of view like a satisfied seal as soon as you've come.

10) No matter how well you know your webcam lover, establish a code of conduct. Any stills or clips taken are for his/her eyes only. You don't want to find yourself on YouTube's Most Viewed list.

2. Make a Woman Ejaculate:

It's the stuff of many a porn-induced fantasy, but although not all women ejaculate, some do. Guys—to find out if your girl is one of the ones who does, you'll need to get very intimately acquainted with her G-spot.

A Road Map

Ask her to lie on her back and open her legs to give you easy access—a pillow under her bum helps too. After you've warmed her up with some oral sex, slide a finger or two into her vagina. Feel along the front wall, a little way past the entrance, until you come to a rough, ridged area that feels different to the touch. It might feel raised and be oval or bean-shaped.

Congratulations—you've made it to the G-spot!

Now continue your good work by crooking your finger in a "come hither" movement and massaging the G. Use firm finger-tip movements—up and down, side-to-side, or plain old static pressure. Ask her what feels best.

The next step is to take her arousal to orgasmic levels
with some clitoral massage. If you find it difficult to multi-
task, ask her to masturbate or apply a vibrator to herself.
Meanwhile, keep giving your undivided attention to her G.

Now all you have to do is hang in there. Combined G-spot
and clitoral stimulation is an efficient way to get her off.
And if she's going to ejaculate, it can happen just before,
during, or after her orgasm. Expect anything from a spurt to
a flood to a few tiny drops of fluid (so tiny as to be undetect-
able). And if it doesn't happen, remember: focus on the
journey not the destination.

Ladies—You Can Help Too

Here are two tips to help out your man:

1) Pee beforehand, this way you can be sure that your "ejaculate" isn't urine.

2) Relax all your vaginal muscles—imagine doing the opposite of a Kegel exercise. In fact, relax to the point where you'd pee if there was any urine in your bladder.

3. Be a Good Dom:

If you want to achieve complete sexual domination over your lover, the first rule is: dress like you mean it. No matter how good your role-playing skills, if you dress in a floral cotton dress or some Gap shorts, you're not going to project that "I can make you do very bad things" vibe.

So think along the lines of leather, latex, buckles, chains, boots, straps, and heels. And rest assured that, although black is an S&M cliché, it always creates the right impression.

To ensure complete obedience from your sub, you also need to get into character.

Talk the Talk

The successful dom never raises his/her voice, always commands rather than requests and never sounds plaintive or says "please" or "thank you." Your voice must resonate with quiet and, occasionally, sadistic authority. Your sub needs to believe that some harsh discipline is never more than a whip crack away. And don't give complex sets of instructions—keep your orders crisp and succinct. For example: "Get on your knees." "Lick me." "Higher."

GET ON YOUR KNEES

Walk the Walk

Learn the body language of power. Always make sure you're looking down at your sub rather than vice versa—ideally they'll be strapped down on the bed and you'll be straddling them in a standing position. Fix your sub in the eye when you speak, and don't smile unless you've perfected the art of the menacing smirk.

Have Your Props on Hand

If you're doing a master/slave-type role-play, and you're threatening punishment, you'll need to deliver. Have your props within easy reach: nipple clamps, whips, cuffs, paddles, bondage tape, and blindfolds are all useful tools for the organized dom. And if you want your sub to stimulate you with a range of sex toys, keep these close as well. As always in games of sex and power, make a prior agreement that if either of you want to quit, you shout a previously agreed code word, known in the business as a "safe word."

4. Find His P-Spot:

These days everyone has heard of the fabled female G-spot, but the good news for guys is that there is a male equivalent: the P-spot, aka the prostate gland.

Anatomy 101

First, a little anatomy. The prostate is a walnut-sized gland that surrounds the urethra—the tube that connects the bladder to the penis, and which also carries semen. The function of the prostate is to contribute towards the seminal fluid, and it secretes an alkaline fluid that makes up to 30 percent of the semen (it helps protect the sperm from the acidic environment of the vagina). There are also some muscles in the prostate that contract during orgasm and help to blast semen out of the penis during ejaculation.

Access Restricted

You can find the prostate between the bladder and the rectum. If you put your finger on the perineum, halfway between a guy's testicles and his anus, and press, you're basically pressing his prostate. But, because there are other bits in the way, you can't really get proper access from the outside.

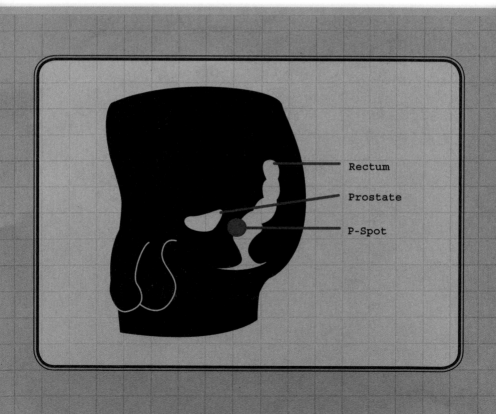

Rectum

Prostate

P-Spot

Pot of Gold

Before going any further you need to know why this little gland is of any erotic interest. It turns out that the prostate is an internal erogenous zone. When a guy is aroused, pressing and rubbing his prostate feels good, and the closer he gets to climax the better it will feel. Time your strokes properly and you can turn an ordinary ejaculation into an earth-shattering orgasm of unprecedented intensity.

Follow the Brown Brick Road

The rainbow that leads to this pot of orgasmic gold is the rectum. While giving a blow- or hand-job, slip a well-lubricated middle finger into his anus, palm towards his front, and push it in about two or three inches. Crook it towards you and rub. As he becomes aroused his prostate will harden and you should be able to feel this. As he nears his climax, rub harder, in time with what you're doing to his penis. Keep massaging the prostate during ejaculation.

Precautions

Remember to observe some precautions—the anus and rectum are highly sensitive and fragile, so always get consent, go slowly, use loads of lubrication, and, on withdrawal, wash your finger(s) before touching anything else.

Accessories

Latex gloves can help fingers to slip in to the anus more easily, and also reassure both partners that exploring fingers are protected against potential encounters with rectal contents (although remember that, unless you are in imminent need of a visit to the toilet, the rectum is usually empty). If either partner is likely to get embarrassed about smell or brown-tinged lube, unscented body wipes can be handy for immediate, discreet hygiene (although fingers should also be scrubbed thoroughly before being used for anything else).

Bear in mind that most guys are not used to being penetrated, and therefore may find it weird or uncomfortable at first. A watered-down version of prostate-stimulation can be achieved by simply massaging the perineum.

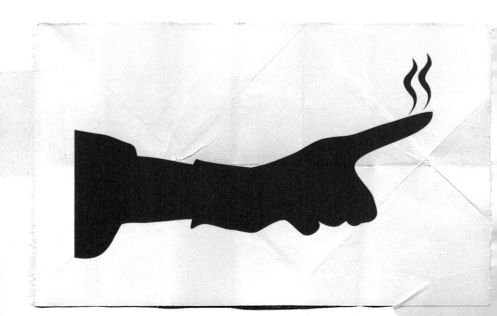

5. Become a Sex Therapist:

Ever considered becoming a sex therapist? There are several good reasons why you should:

- You get to listen to other people's sexual problems all day (which is guaranteed to make you feel much better about your own).

- Some of your clients will be nymphomaniacs, sex addicts, or just people who get laid more than you, so you could pick up a few hints and, at the very least, hear loads of raunchy stories.

- It could help you to get laid—no! not with your clients (that would be highly unethical and possibly illegal)—but with everyone else. People always assume that sex therapists must be great in bed because they know so much about it.

- You could even make some money.

The Hard Way

There are two main routes into sex therapy—which one you take depends on how ethical you are. Route One is for people who have consciences. Unfortunately it involves considerable effort, as you would do well to win accreditation from one of the recognized organizations for sex therapists, such as the American Association of Sexuality Educators, Counselors and Therapists in the US, or the British Association for Sexual and Relationship Therapy in the UK. To achieve this you would usually need to have a degree of some sort, followed by more specialized training in psychology, psychotherapy, counseling, social work, or healthcare. Then you could try a specialized graduate training program in human sexuality. You'll probably need to go through a long process involving self-analysis, mentoring, workshops, and academic work.

The Easy Way

Sound like a lot of effort? Well, if you have the ethics of a weasel, you could take Route Two, which is predicated on the fact that sex therapy is not a legally regulated profession. In other words, there is nothing to stop you putting up a sign in your window saying "Sex Therapist" and sticking an advertisement in the local paper offering your services to all, even though you know nothing about therapy and less about sex.

Bluffer's Guide

Whether or not you get caught depends on how good you are bullshitting. Avoid getting snagged by using this handy bluffer's guide to giving good therapy:

1. Look relaxed but authoritative. It helps to wear a jacket.

2. See your client in a room decorated in subdued bohemian fashion, as if to say, "Hey, I'm a man/woman of the world, but don't worry, I'm not a hippy."

3. Ask questions like "Would you say your sexual needs are being fulfilled?"

4. Repeat their answers back to them as questions. For example, "And why do you think your sexual needs are not being fulfilled?"

5. If in doubt, say: "And how does that make you feel?"

6. If a client challenges your credentials/ability/ value for money, use the universal safety line: "I'm sorry you feel that way, let's explore why you're really saying that."

6. Perform Auto-Fellatio:

Auto-fellatio is the technical term for sucking your own dick. Don't believe it's possible? Look on Wikipedia and see for yourself. Estimates of the number of men who can auto-fellate are around 1 percent or less of the population (the criteria for success being the ability to suck or lick your own penis, rather than just touch it with the tip of your tongue). But people who can do it describe it as the ultimate form of masturbation.

Rising to the Challenge

Most men have tried auto-fellatio at least once in their lives, but the overwhelming majority will find that nature has not gifted them in this way. In order to succeed, you will need to be highly flexible or have a very long penis—ideally both. Men with particularly long penises may be able to simply bend over and fit the end of their penis into their mouth.

A notable example is the legendary porn star Ron Jeremy, who first came to prominence in the 1981 porn film *Lips*, in which he attracts the attentions of a passing jogger by pleasuring himself in this way. Jeremy is pudgy, but he is also quite short (making for less distance between cock and mouth). Crucially, he has a 10-inch penis. Failing such gifts, you will need to work on your flexibility through yoga and stretching.

Self-sucking Positions

There are a number of positions you can adopt in pursuit of auto-fellatio. The most common is "The Plow," in which you lie on your back and put your legs over your head. In the "Over Easy" position, you sit upright but grab your thighs and pull your head downwards towards your crotch. The same technique but in a standing position is known as "The Stork." In the "X" position you cross your legs behind your head and lean forward towards your penis.

WARNING: Don't attempt any of these positions if you have any back, bone, muscle, or joint problems. But do not despair, for according to Gary Griffin, author of *The Art of Auto-Fellatio*, "A much greater number [of men] would be able to fellate themselves if they were to undergo a program of proper conditioning, stretching, and yoga exercises over a period of months."

7. Behave like an Eighteenth Century Rake:

A rake was a rich young man of the 18th century, who dissipated his youth and fortune on gambling, drinking and, above all, womanizing. "Rake" was short for "Rakehell", a reference to the libidinous libertine's likely afterlife location. In order to qualify as a rake, it was necessary to be young, unmarried, and in possession of a vast quantity of money.

You, Sir, Are No Gentleman!

Despite attracting official opprobrium the rake was the envy of every red-blooded man and the fantasy of every woman. To adopt the persona of an 18th-century rake simply follow these steps:

1. Come into an inheritance or endowment that generates an annual income of at least $400,000. On no account must you work for your cash—you won't have time for anything as plebeian as a job.

2. Acquire a plush townhouse in an exclusive uptown locale. Decorate with silks, Persian rugs, and antique furniture.

3. Rise at noon, or later if possible. Breakfast on quails' eggs and champagne.

4. Go for a ride in a fashionable park. (Yes, you will need horses and, if possible, a carriage. Alternatively, a convertible Ferrari or Aston Martin will do.)

5. At 8pm, meet up with other rakes for dinner at an obscenely expensive restaurant, preferably in a private room. Around midnight, move on to an exclusive watering hole, hole up in the VIP section, and blow the equivalent of $40 of 18th-century money on booze. Doesn't sound like much? That's $4,000 dollars today!

6. Either collect a suitable number of young women (ideally of impeccable breeding) for a party in a hotel room or private members' only club, or visit a high-class brothel.

7. If at all possible, corrupt (i.e. take the virginity of) the most proper young lady you can find—daughters of high-ranking ministers, foreign ambassadors, and European royalty are best.

8. Laugh callously if she claims to be in love with you, and then pass her onto your friends.

9. Return home at dawn; sleep late.

10. Repeat until ruined, syphilitic, sclerotic or killed in a duel.

8. Have Remote Control Sex:

Ever fancied getting your partner off without having to lift more than a finger?

Advances in battery and radio control technology mean that it's now possible to drive your partner wild without even touching him or her. With a new breed of remotely controlled sex toys you can exert a highly dis-crete brand of erotic mastery over your man or woman—espe-cially in public places and/or crowded situations. This technology is also tailor-made for phone sex and helps couples to stay sexually con-nected when they're a long way apart.

Play the Vibes

First you need to acquire a remotely controlled sex toy. The easiest ones to find are "bullet vibes": small vibrators the size and shape of a pebble or egg, designed to fit discretely into your underwear—or even inside you. The "vibes" are rigged so that they can be activated to give short bursts of vibration in response to a text message or phone call. If you look hard enough, you may be able to find more ambitious types of remote control sex technology, like cell-phone-operated dildos.

Choose Your Moment

The real thrill comes not so much from the stimulation provided by the toy, but by handing over total control of your erogenous zones to your partner... and by the knowledge that he/she can zap you with a jolt of secret stimulation wherever and whenever he/she chooses. For the controlling partner, the thrill of furtive, hands-free fondling can be a tremendous turn-on. Plus you can derive immense satisfaction from watching your partner struggle to keep their cool in the middle of a crowded bar or commuter train while you remorselessly trigger their vibrator.

Phone Sex 2.0

Such devices are also perfect for adding an extra, physical dimension to phone sex—the "vibes" can be rigged to buzz the whole time you are on the phone to one another. Buy a matching set of remote control sex toys and you can delight one another without even being on the same continent.

9. Get a Sex Change:

Sexual reassignment surgery (SRS) is not undertaken lightly—in order to qualify you have to meet a whole load of requirements, pass a lot of assessments, and go through a number of stages.

The guidelines that determine whether you can switch gender differ from country to country. The definitive guide is usually taken to be the Harry Benjamin International Gender Dysphasia Association's Standards of Care for Gender Identity Disorders (HBIGDA-SOCGID for short). This is basically a list of the things you should do before getting a sex change. After all, SRS will have an impact on every aspect of your life, from your personal relationships to your career prospects, not to mention your entire worldview and psyche.

First Steps

First you have to show that you can comfortably adapt to living as if you were a member of the opposite gender. You'll need to be doing things such as cross-dressing, non-surgical body modification (e.g., hair removal in the case of men), engaging in appropriate activities, and generally adopting a different lifestyle. You also have to educate yourself about the issues and the process, and show that you've considered the wider impact of the change on your relationships and career.

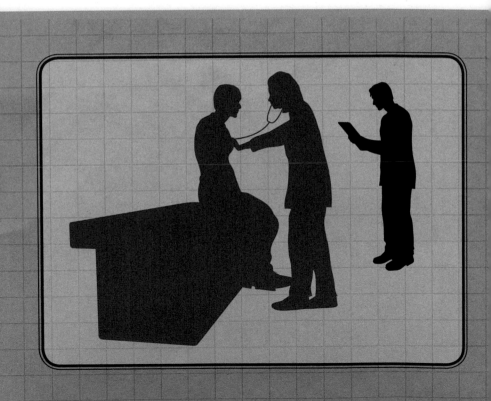

Bring on the Hormones

The next stage is non-surgical intervention—mainly hormone treatment. This is a serious step in itself with potentially irreversible consequences. You will need to show doctors and psychologists that you are making progress with the psychological issues caused by being gender dysphoric (the clinical term for gender identity confusion/dissatisfaction). You also have to be free of substance abuse, depression, and other mental health problems.

Under the Knife

After successfully living as the opposite gender and being on hormone therapy for a year, you'll be eligible for the next stage, although, again, you will need to prove you're psychologically capable. Unless you're lucky enough to be in one of the few countries where the state will pay, you'll also need lots of money—between $3,000 and $100,000, depending on how far you want to go. Removal of the testicles and penis and the creation of a simulated vagina, or the removal of breasts and the creation of a simulated penis, are the most extreme steps. On top of this, most SRSers opt to have cosmetic surgery such as changes to their features done.

10. Make Fake Jism:

No home should be without a ready supply of fake jism; it's great for role-play, fantasy, and sex games, and is essential for anyone planning to make their own porn film.

There are several recipes you can use, but all have the same goal—to recreate the essential characteristics of male love juice: consistency, color, and flavor. You're after a fluid that's viscous, will set quickly on dispersal into a jelly-like fluid, and has the correct milky color. As far as flavor goes, it depends on how much of a perfectionist you are. You could take the view that this is your chance to improve on nature by producing something sweet or fruit-flavored, or you could try to capture the unique taste of the real thing (salt and crushed aspirin are said to achieve this).

Even Better Than the Real Thing

To recreate the consistency of real jism, the fake stuff needs something that will thicken water into a gel-like substance. Proteins and starch can both accomplish this, which is why egg white and cornstarch/arrowroot are common ingredients... but you need to be aware of the health issues.

Recipe 1

This is for people who don't mind a high risk of yeast infections or salmonella.

Ingredients:

1 cup/250ml water

1 raw egg white

2 tablespoons cornstarch

1 tablespoon sweet condensed milk

1 pinch salt

(Scale up contents proportionately for more fake jism.)

Method: Dissolve the cornstarch in water while heating on a stove. Add a pinch of salt. Stir until all the starch is dissolved. Allow to cool completely—this is very important. If not cooled the egg will cook when you add it. Add the egg and the milk, and whisk until smooth. Apply liberally.

Warning: Raw egg may contain salmonella; applying sugary foodstuffs to genitals is a recipe for yeast infections.

Recipe 2

This is for the more safety conscious.

Ingredients:

1 cup/250 ml water

2 tablespoons arrowroot

1 tablespoon powdered egg white

1 pinch salt

(Scale up contents proportionately for more fake jism.)

Method: As above, but with arrowroot in place of cornstarch. Add artificial sweetener if you want something sweet. Remember that the longer you cook the arrowroot mixture, the thicker and more viscous it will become, so dilute to taste.

Warning: Even this recipe still carries a risk of yeast infection, so use with care and try to avoid getting any on your mucous membranes.

Application Process

To apply the concoction created from either recipe, you can either buy a sex toy with a built in bladder/pump, or simply use a squirty ketchup bottle. Use immediately to reduce the chances of the mixture going bad.

11. Write Erotica:

Erotica is a burgeoning but misunderstood market in publishing. It's perfectly suited to e-publishing (writing sold on the Internet and delivered electronically), which circumvents the problem of embarrassed buyers being seen with an actual dirty book. And these days there's real money in it. But not everyone can do it. Here are eight rules to writing titillating erotica:

Rule 1: You must be comfortable with sex; doing it, talking about it, writing about it. If you're not comfortable, this will show in your writing, which will be awkward and restrained and ring false.

Rule 2: Erotica is not the same as porn. It's also different from romance fiction, lying somewhere between the two. Erotica is upfront and explicit about sex, but has real plots, characters, and feelings. In practice, erotica is hard to pin down as a specific genre, because it's a great fan of genre-busting. One important sub-genre is "romantica"—romance fiction with much more graphic sex and language than normal.

Rule 3: Your story must have some—and ideally all—of the following: real characters, a real plot, and a properly realized setting. However, this doesn't mean it has to happen in the real world. Some of the most popular erotica is set in fantasy worlds with vampires, elves, etc.

Rule 4: Write real sex, not porno sex. Characters shouldn't necessarily come the moment a cock goes in, or bang away unrepentantly like a machine with a ramrod straight dick. Not every character needs a 10-inch prick or massive tits (although a character with both might be interesting).

Rule 5: Follow the rules of good writing. Use all five senses in describing things, especially sex. Be specific. Show (through action), don't simply tell. But add erotic elements—be sensual and bold. Also don't be coy, crass, or overly purple.

Rule 6: Get an erotic thesaurus, otherwise your writing will quickly become repetitive. But use commonsense and try not to be clinical. "He intromitted her vulva," is unlikely to ring anyone's bells.

Rule 7: The essence of erotica is that sex and the story are integral to one another. If your story works without the sex, or the sex is independent of the story, it's not proper erotica.

Rule 8: Avoid clichés and be truthful—about sex, character, motivation, plot, etc.,—even when you're writing fantasy.

12. Make a Backdoor Entrance:

In case you haven't worked out this transparent euphemism, we're talking about anal sex here. Yes, sodomy, buggery, cornholing, rear-ending, getting the brown glove treatment, drilling for oil on the Moon. Anal sex is something that everyone can do—male and female, straight and gay. There are some health implications, but if you follow basic precautions they need not prevent you from adding a whole new dimension to your sex life.

Anal Is Forgiven

The first thing to note is that anal sex has had a bad rap. It is condemned by major religions and is actually still illegal in many parts of the world, including several states in the US. So if you live in one of these places, do NOT do this, we are NOT promoting any such activity, you NEVER heard of this book, all right? If, on the other hand, you live in the 21st century, why shouldn't you engage in a potentially pleasurable activity? Stimulation of zones that are erogenous but not reproductive is no problem when it comes to nibbling

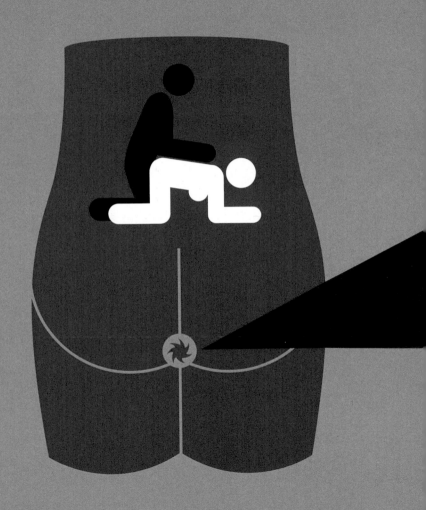

earlobes, caressing breasts, or sucking toes—and the anus, which is highly sensitive, can be as erogenous as any of these. For men it has the added bonus of providing a route to the prostate, the nearest male equivalent to the female G-spot—see page 17. (These are all good arguments to use on a reluctant partner, by the way.)

5 Simple Rules for Ass Fun

You can practice anal sex with a finger, multiple fingers, a penis, sex toys, and even the tongue (although this has particular health considerations). Follow these important rules at all times:

1. Never attempt anal sex without explicit permission from your partner. Surprising them could be dangerous, painful, ruinous to your relationship, and potentially criminal.

2. Be hygienic. Ideally men should wear a condom, and partners should ensure their rectums are clean and clear of feces. Never penetrate the vagina with the same object/ member that has just been used to penetrate the anus. Clean objects/members immediately after anal sex.

3. Be gentle and use lubrication—lots of it, ideally a water-based lubricant such as KY jelly. The anus can be tight and the rectal walls are thin, sensitive, and easily torn.

4. The partner being penetrated should push back onto the penetrator, not the other way around.

5. Relax. Stop immediately if there is pain, strong discomfort, or bleeding.

Warning: If anal sex is followed by pain, problems with bowel movements, bleeding from the anus, or bloody/black feces, consult a doctor immediately.

13. Deal with an Obscene Phone Call:

Obscene phone calls can range from being an almost amusing nuisance to a terrifying ordeal of ongoing harassment. Some people choose to respond proactively, for example by buying a very loud whistle and blowing it at full strength down the phone to burst the caller's stupid pervy eardrums. This is a Bad Idea. For one thing, there's probably an amplitude limiter on the phone network, so it would be impossible to inflict a damagingly loud noise across a phone line, and in fact the only person whose hearing would suffer would be your own.

Stay Cool

More importantly, this is exactly the kind of rise that a pervert phone harasser is seeking, because what gets them off is hearing you get upset, agitated and out of control. Control is all important; the obscene caller is aroused or excited by the sense of being in control, but the best thing you can do is remember that you are in control. So don't get mad. Do the opposite: be calm and rational and follow these six important steps.

1. **Hang up!** This should be your first response. As soon as you hear something inappropriate, put the phone down. Do this every time they ring back, without exception. The worst thing you can do is engage with the caller, even if it is to ask them what is wrong with their pathetic lives or why they can't get a girlfriend. Don't ask them questions, and never answer any of theirs.

2. **Remain calm.** The caller wants to hear you freak out, get angry or get scared. Do not give them the satisfaction.

3. **Most callers are random** and easily discouraged by hang-ups. If the caller persists, call the police. It is a criminal offence to make obscene or harassing phone calls.

4. **Call your telephone service provider.** They may be able to prevent calls from that number coming through to you; identify the caller; ensure that caller ID is always displayed so you can screen your calls; and, if necessary, change your number and take you ex-directory.

5. **Keep a log of the time and date of all calls.** This may be important as evidence and in helping to trace the caller.

6. **On no account respond to the question** "What are you wearing?" with an elaborate description of your crotchless French maid's uniform.

14. Ejaculate Internally:

Learn how to come without coming and you can have multiple orgasms, rapid recovery, and enhanced life energy.

The Small Death

This is the claim of the Chinese Taoists, who believe—to paraphrase a famous song—that every time you lose your wad you die a little. According to this ancient tradition semen is a "vital substance," chock-full of life energy or chi, and ejaculation means that you are losing some of your life energy. Taoists call ejaculation "the small death." One of the secrets of Taoist super-sex is the technique for internal ejaculation, or "injaculation."

The Million-Dollar Point

The key to injaculation is to apply pressure to a point on the perineum (the zone between your balls and your anus) called the Jen Mao point, more colloquially known as the "million-dollar point" because of its supposed health benefits. Taoists claim that preventing the emission of semen prolongs your life, and improves your sex life by helping you to recover and regain your erection more quickly, and even to keep your erection and experience multiple orgasms.

For Taoists the Jen Mao point is an acupressure point affecting the flow of chi around your body, but in fact it is the slightly fleshy part of the perineum where the urethra—the tube that carries semen from the prostate to the penis—can be closed off with pressure, applied by pressing hard on the spot. Locate your million-dollar point by probing your perineum just in front of your anus; it should yield slightly to pressure. Supposedly pressing here just before you come can block the urethra and prevent semen from coming out.

Don't Try This at Home

The Taoists believed that if you pressed on exactly the right spot the semen was simply reabsorbed by your system, boosting your health all round, but modern medicine is skeptical and warns that attempting injaculation can be harmful on several fronts. Firstly, the semen is not reabsorbed but simply sent back the wrong way—up the urethra and into the bladder. This can increase the chance of infection of both urethra and bladder, and it might even damage the sphincters and valves that are supposed to ensure one-way traffic. More to the point, the perineum is sensitive and easy to damage. Since there is no actual evidence for any of the positive claims made by the Taoists, you're probably better off not even trying this.

15. Have Gourmet Sex:

Sex is supposed to be a feast for the senses, but some people go one step further.

Sex and eating are both sensuous activities that give great pleasure, so why not combine them? Food can be sensuous through texture and taste, in tactile, visual, olfactory, and gustatory fashion—just like your sex organs! There are a number of ways you can whip up a sexual banquet or incorporate food into sex, in what is known as "food play", or, to be technical, sitophilia.

Coating, Dripping, and Licking

Pouring and rubbing fluids over your own body or your partner's is sensuous fun and can help to supercharge erotic massage. If you make the fluid something edible and tasty you can add the pleasure of licking each other to the equation. Chocolate sauce is a popular choice, and milk is an option that can look like rivers of cum (which some people find arousing).

Seaweed Sake

A specific example of this is the rare Japanese practice of Wakamezake, or "seaweed sake", in which a woman presses her legs tightly together to form a triangular depression between the thighs and the mons pubis. Sake is poured onto her chest and flows down into this natural cup, from where her partner drinks it. Her pubic hair drifting in the sake is said to resemble fronds of seaweed in the sea.

Sexual Banquet

Some foods are said to be particularly erotic or aphrodisiac—like strawberries, dipped in chocolate and fed to each other—and these can be incorporated into sex play, with teasing, stroking of erogenous zones, and eating off one another.

Nyotaimori

An extreme version of this, which mixes sitophilia with bondage/dom-sub elements, is the practice of nyotaimori ("female body presentation", known as nantaimori if practiced with men). This is where a naked woman is used as a serving platter for sushi. She may be completely shaved, and be expected to remain still and exposed for long periods of time, while diners either ignore or tease her. It is probably more common in Western media reports than in actual Japanese practice.

16. Compile a Sex Library:

"The best effect of any book is that it excites the reader to self-activity," said Thomas Carlyle, although possibly he didn't have wanking in mind. Erotic books have a long and distinguished pedigree, and nothing tells the world that you are a sexy sophisticate like a lewd library of lasciviousness.

Keep It Old School

Porn mags are frankly déclassé, and they certainly won't impress any potential partners. If you really want to convince him or her that you are a suave sybarite—a creature of cosmopolitan passions and hip hedonism—you need to display a bit of class, and what better way than with the hand-tooled leather and crimson bindings of a volume of pure, unbridled, old-fashioned filth? Nothing says "class" like antique erotic literature, so if at all possible, line your bookshelves with the stuff.

You will, however, need lots of money because, owing to a recent fashion for collecting antique erotica, such books (which by their nature were generally very rare) can cost thousands of dollars. A first edition of *Les Liaisons Dangereuses*, for instance, will set you back $25,000, while a first edition of De Sade's *Justine* is worth $40,000.

The Joy of Texts

If this is beyond your budget, don't worry. The exploding market for erotica means that you can buy all sorts of titles in sex shops, some lingerie boutiques, and, above all, online. Try Delectus Books, a web-based erotic bookseller where you can pick up treasures like *The Mistress and the Slave,* or the classic *Story of O*. Experiment with some of the erotic comics on the market. Comic artist Erich von Gotha is like a latter-day graphic De Sade.

For Your Eyes Only

Think carefully about where you're going to put your library of the licentious. Bawdy bibliophiles may appreciate shelf-loads of sophisticated smut, but your mother-in-law may not be so impressed. A secluded study or den is best, preferably lined with rich wood and leather paneling, decorated with exotic rugs and ethnic fetishes from around the world, redolent of expensive sherry and Cuban cigars. Failing that—keep them in a box under your bed.

17. Practice Kama Sutra:

Use your mastery of the *Kama Sutra* to knock your partner off his/her feet (and put them behind his/her head).

The Good Stuff

The *Kama Sutra* is an ancient Indian compendium of texts about the arts of love and sex. Contrary to popular belief, only one section of it details outrageous sexual positions, and it has nothing to do with tantra. Most of it concerns the proper instruction for a high caste young man entering into adult life and dealing with wives, courtesans, etc. But who cares about any of that?! You want to know about the Congress of the Cow, don't you?

Assume the Position

As far as saucing things up in the bedroom, what really counts are the weird and wonderful sexual positions for which the *Kama*

Sutra is famous. The Congress of the Cow, for instance, is a standing position in which the woman bends at the waist until her hands are flat on the floor and the man grasps her hips and enters her from behind. Why this is bovine is unclear. Perhaps its original creator was anticipating that you would have to suffer from mad cow disease before you'd try anything so silly.

Kama Chameleon

Rather than waste time actually reading the *Kama Sutra*, just follow this quick bluffer's guide:

• **Use a lot of candles, silk sheets, cushions, incense, essential oils, etc.—you know, like they did in ancient India.**

• **Have some god-awful sitar music playing in the background.**

• **Wear sandals.**

• **Refer to the penis and vagina as the lingam and the yoni.**

• **Talk a lot about chakras and kundalini energy, even though they have nothing to do with the *Kama Sutra*.**

• **Make up a strange position and tell your partner it's called the Cheesecloth of the Drooping Ibis, or something. If you are really clever you can incorporate watching TV or eating a sandwich. If your partner objects simply tell them: "Hey—the purpose of *Kama Sutra* is the perfection of kama, the pursuit of pleasure, one of the four purusharthas of life, and a sacred duty. Now pass the ketchup."**

18. Tell if She's Had an Orgasm:

Sex manuals and *Cosmo* tell you that there is more to sex than orgasms, but in the real world all men know that there is only one true measure of sexual success and satisfaction. If she didn't hit the high note, it'll end on a low note.

Spotter's Guide

Having said which, it is often hard to tell the difference between generic moaning and the specifically orgasmic variety. So how do you know when it's OK to reach your own climax? Use this expert spotter's guide to help you. She's probably had an orgasm if...

• **She says, "Oh my god I'm coming." Alas, women are rarely this helpful. But vocalizations can be a good tip, especially if your partner is normally silent/non-verbal during sex.**

• **She gets "flush" (redness) across her chest. This is a common reaction to extreme arousal.**

- She has a sequence of increasingly rapid, shallow breaths leading to an abrupt cessation of breathing and extreme tension of her whole body for a second or more, followed by auditory and physical signs of "letting go." Women often describe the sensation of orgasm as a build-up of tension until a tipping point is reached where everything is suddenly released in a flood.

- She squeezes her eyes shut and screws up her face in an expression that would not look out of place in a torture victim.

- Her vagina contracts rhythmically.

- Inarticulate writhing, clawing, and convulsions are accompanied by uncontrollable moaning, gasping, and screaming. Do not make the mistake of thinking that all or even most women will orgasm like this, however. Real life isn't like porn.

- There is a gush of fluid from her vagina. This could be urine, but it may also be female ejaculation (see page 10). Again, this is extremely rare.

- She wants to have sex with you again.

19. Have Coitus à Mammilia:

Coitus à mammilia is a fancy term for "titty-f**king"—rubbing the penis between the breasts. This act is also said to be mazophallate (meaning "penetrating between the breasts"). To be honest this one is more for the guys—women don't have too many nerve endings between their breasts, so any pleasure they're likely to receive is vicarious.

Size Matters

For successful coitus à mammilia, a minimum amount of cleavage is probably necessary. There are several ways you can do it. The woman could kneel in front of a seated man, squeeze her breasts around his penis and rub/bounce them up and down, but this may be awkward and cause discomfort for her (plus it's not healthy for breasts to be bounced around too vigorously).

The better alternative is probably for the woman to lie on her back while the man straddles her chest and leans forward so that his penis is between her breasts. While she squeezes them together to give some friction, he can thrust back and forth. Lubrication may help.

Pearl Necklace

Successful technique is likely to be rewarded with a "pearl necklace"—ejaculation onto the upper chest and neck. But coitus à mammilia isn't just for male mammagymnophiliacs (people who get aroused by female breasts). A woman can also masturbate her clitoris and labia against a female partner's breasts and nipples.

Coitus A-Go-Go

There are many other "coitus á..." options. For instance, coitus á unda is sex involving water (see page 58). Coitus à cheval—sex on horseback—is an ancient practice in horse-centred cultures. The rocking motion of the horse (or any other beast of burden) can be used to guide or enhance copulation. Sex games that mimic coitus á cheval are also an important part of dom-sub culture, such as ones where "slaves" are bridled and ridden.

Coitus interfermoris is the thrusting of the penis between the thighs of the partner. It is a form of safe sex and was traditionally used as birth control in the ancient Levant (according to the Jewish Talmud). It was also popular with Greek homosexual couples.

20. Have an Affair:

Adultery is a fact of life—in fact according to a branch of evolutionary science called sociobiology, we've evolved specifically to be adulterous. The rationale is that men produce so much semen that it's in their favor to spread it around as widely as possible, effectively planting their seed in other men's allotments. For women, the evolutionary motive is to secure a partner who will provide for you, meanwhile "shopping around" for the best semen to produce a child.

Securing a Liaison

Finding someone to have an affair with is a bit like looking for a date—you've got to put yourself out there a bit. You need to get into situations where you'll naturally meet a wide selection of the opposite sex. Here are some tips to find a willing affair partner:

- **If you have attractive/lonely neighbors, start working from home.**

• Travel a lot for work. Spend your evenings looking available in the hotel bar.

• Go to a lot of conferences. Illicit liaisons between attendees are practically compulsory.

• If you have a susceptible colleague/boss/assistant/ office cleaner, start working late. Arrange to stay behind to help with "that important report."

• Fathers—take your kids to school. It's mostly moms who do the school run. Mothers—take your kids to sports practices. In both these cases there is a window of opportunity when the kids are gone but you and the (mostly opposite sex) other parents are in the same place.

Dos and Don'ts

Do shower after having sex. Do check your pockets carefully. Do get your cover story straight. Right, that's the dos out of the way. The don'ts are far more important. Do not:

- let your lover leave sexy underwear hanging off your furniture

- use your credit card to pay for flowers, champagne, and hotel rooms if your partner is likely to see the bill

- exchange love bites

- let your lover call you at home

- leave your cell phone around for your partner to look at

- exchange emails from your home computer

- cry out your lover's name during sex with your husband/wife

- start buying uncharacteristic presents for your husband/wife

- pause, while discussing colleagues/ PTA members/ etc., when you come to the name of your lover

21. Have Sex in Water:

Perhaps you're on a romantic island vacation, maybe you've just met a hottie at a pool party, or possibly you're just taking a relaxing bath together. You're splashing around, naked or nearly naked, slipping and sliding over one another. What could be more natural than engaging in a bit of albutophilia (sex in the water)? Renowned pervert and emperor of Rome, Tiberius Caesar, was particularly fond of undinism (yes, "sex in the water" again), and employed young boys he called his "minnows" to swim up from beneath him and suck and nibble his genitals. There's even a whacky but influential theory that humans evolved from aquatic apes, so perhaps nautical nookie is what nature intended.

Water, Water Everywhere

Ironically, the abundance of fluid involved poses serious problems for lubrication, which means that coitus à unda—as it's also known—is difficult and not always advisable. Pleasurable intercourse depends on the lubrication produced by the vagina, and water, whether fresh or salty, may dilute this or wash it away, so you may need to augment the natural supply with some artificial help. KY jelly is probably best, but who brings a tube with them to the beach? In the bath you may be tempted to use soap or bubblebath, but these can irritate his and particularly her genitals.

Contraception Issues

Water is particularly problematic for contraception. Putting on a condom is tough when you're underwater, and it's also much more likely to come off (plus there's uncertainty about how condoms react to salt or chlorine). The same problems apply to diaphragms, spermicide, and sponges. On top of all this, you have to worry about water hygiene (although it's a myth that swimming pool chlorine is especially bad for genitals, or that getting water into the vagina is dangerous). Oh, and did we mention, having sex in a public place is illegal?

So the bottom line for sex in the water is probably don't do it. If you can't resist, however, make sure that:

a) she's very turned on and very wet

b) there's no chance of anyone coming across your aquatic antics

c) you've considered your contraception options

d) you're not bobbing around in some sewage outflow

22. Cure Impotence:

Popping a pill is for wimps. Real men treat causes, not just symptoms.

Feeling Droopy?

Erectile dysfunction (ED), as it is technically known, can have devastating effects on the male psyche, affecting self-esteem, self-image, libido, gender identity, and mental health in general. Because it's so embarrassing to admit to, few people realize just how common it is. Almost all men will experience it at some point in their lives, and it affects as many as 40 percent of men over 65 who are not in good health.

This is why sildenafil (better known as Viagra®) is the biggest development in male medicine since goat glands (a common therapy for impotence in the early 20th century). But PDE5 inhibitors (the class of drug that includes Viagra®), although overwhelmingly the initial treatment of choice in modern ED therapy, are not necessarily the answer.

In the Heart or in the Head?

ED can have physical or psychological causes (or a mixture of both). It can be an indicator of serious health problems, such as diabetes, cardiovascular disease, or depression, in which case treatment of the underlying cause is at least as important as treating ED, which is simply a symptom. But ED can be entirely mental, in which case psychotherapy could resolve the issue without recourse to drugs (which have side effects and may be harmful).

So your first step should be to speak to the doctor and get checked up. If your ED has a physical cause, this can be addressed. If it is psychological, you can discuss treatment options. If you can obtain an erection at all (for instance, while masturbating or while asleep), then the causes are probably mental.

The Stamp Test

Antique sex manuals offer an unlikely method for determining whether or not you get sleeping erections: stick postage stamps around the shaft of your penis. If the perforations are torn in the morning, this indicates that, as is normal, you have experienced erections during the night.

De-stressing

The leading cause of psychologically-induced ED is probably stress. Modern life allows too little time for partners to relax together, and if you are tired and anxious you are much more likely to suffer impotence. So one important treatment is to learn to de-stress and fight anxiety. Psychotherapies such as CBT(Cognitive Behavioral Therapy) are particularly effective at helping to combat distracting thoughts that cause some men to lose erections.

In Praise of Viagra

Having said all of which, PDE5 inhibitors have proved themselves to be remarkably effective at treating all kinds of impotence with relatively few side effects. They are even effective at overcoming psychologically-induced ED, and the boost to self-esteem that this generates can be therapeutic in itself. For some sufferers, simply the confidence they derive from having some pills available can be curative. There is evidence that they can also help women in boosting sexual responsiveness and, as a consequence, libido. (If you can't afford Viagra® or your doctor won't prescribe it to you, try making your own aphrodisiac—see pages 140 and 142.)

23. Have Sex in an Elevator:

You know the scene—the two stars of the movie, who pretend that they can't stand each other but actually can't wait to get down and dirty, bicker all the way into the elevator. But then as soon as the doors slide shut and the little bell goes "ding" they fall on each other with passionate kisses and desperate tearing off of clothes. Cut to elevator reaching first floor where crowd of unsuspecting stiffs are waiting to board; will they be confronted with our hero and heroine rutting like weasels in undignified fashion? Of course not—when the doors open they're somehow back on their feet, with only their disheveled hair and clothes and general air of smugness giving them away.

Looks like fun, doesn't it? Only in real life it's not so easy. In order to pull it off you'll have to do some or all of the following:

• Make sure you pick an elevator that is either a) very very slow; or b) only stops at the first floor and the 150th floor.

• Have sex incredibly quickly. As in 90 seconds from start to finish.

• Wait until after hours, when no one else is using the elevators.

• Rehearse rapid removal of key items of clothing and undoing of zippers, buttons, etc., so that when you're "in theatre" you can accomplish this at high speed.

• Try not to lean against the buttons, or you may find yourself making unscheduled stops.

• Avoid elevators with operators (unless that's who you want to have sex with).

• Think twice about hitting the emergency stop button—this only works in films. In real life you will end up being hauled out by the Fire and Rescue service and fined huge sums of money.

• Ensure that when the elevator reaches its next stop, at which a crowd of people are waiting to enter, that you and your partner are fully clothed and have adopted insouciant but ultimately unconvincing positions of innocence, with only your disheveled hair and general air of extreme self-satisfaction giving the game away. That and the fact that the elevator will smell of semen and sweat.

• Be careful of elevators with concertina-gate style doors, as you could easily get something caught.

24. Shoot Your Own Porn:

Ever fancied yourself as a porn star, or dreamed of being an erotic auteur? Even if you've never fancied being named Randy Bigwan or Ivana Shagalot for a day, you can still enjoy the erotic benefits of some filmic filth. Filming yourself alone or with a partner can bring an erotic charge to the bedroom through introducing drama and theatre, the thrill of transgression and the knowledge that you can rewind and watch it again. Plus you have the option of keeping it as a record of your sexual prime; something to titillate you in the years to come.

Flatter Yourself

The camera can be cruel so it is important to do everything you can to present yourself—literally—in the best light.

• **Avoid unflattering angles. Try not to shoot from below, as this will emphasize flab, double-chins, bellies, etc.**

• **Use low, soft-lighting if possible. Harsh and bright lights, especially** fluorescent ones, will be too revealing and unflattering. Shooting in night-vision mode can help to conceal imperfections.

• Use clothes and props to help you. Lingerie, nighties, etc., can be used to good effect to cover up parts of your body that make you self-conscious. So can cushions, throws, and other bedding.

• Avoid unflattering positions. For instance, bending forwards at the waist is a surefire way to accentuate flab. Sitting astride someone while arching your back is more likely to be flattering. Don't be afraid to tense muscles, suck in your gut, etc.

Shooting Mode

A tripod is obviously handy if you are filming yourself alone, and can also allow you and a partner to concentrate on what you're doing and forget about the camera. But using the camera in hand-held mode adds both an element of first-person verité to the film and introduces a voyeuristic/exhibitionist element to the sex.

Erase and Rewind?

Consider whether you need to keep your sex tape after the immediate erotic charge of filming and watching it once has faded. If you erase, you limit the chances of it falling into the wrong hands/being used for the wrong ends. If you decide to keep a sex tape, or send a film you've made to someone, be very careful and very certain that you can trust the other person not to circulate the tape or use it in spite.

25. Delay Ejaculation for an Hour:

Unfortunately the primary sources of sex education for men are porn and smutty talk in the playground, so it's hardly surprising that they think the be all and end all of sexual accomplishment is being able to stay rock hard for hours on end. Having said which, knowing how to hold off your own climax until you've given your partner several of their own is a useful trick to be able to pull off occasionally, so here's an instant guide to delaying ejaculation.

Ejaculatory Incompetence

As this is a responsible book, it behooves us to point out that delayed ejaculation is actually a common sexual problem, known in such cases as retarded ejaculation (RE) or even, in the typically damning medical terminology of yesteryear, "ejaculatory incompetence." RE is no laughing matter. It can destroy relationships and cause infertility. Equally priapism –an erection sustained until it becomes injurious—is a serious problem, the risk of which should be borne in mind before embarking on ill-conceived experiments with self-medication.

No Ejaculation Without Sensation

OK, it's not quite what the Founding Fathers fought for, but one way to avoid ejaculating is to use tactics employed to treat premature ejaculation. These include extra-thick condoms, lubrication with mild anesthetic, and similar techniques to reduce sensation in the penis and thus make it harder to reach orgasm. Unfortunately this is also a good way to ruin sex, making this the equivalent of throwing the baby out with the bathwater.

Who's on First?

A tried and trusted technique used by generations of men is to think about something else when nearing ejaculation— something non-sexual, like baseball. The risk here is that you will find yourself fantasizing about home runs instead of concentrating on the matter at hand. Woody Allen had a gag about this in his early stand-up routine:

The two of us are making love violently, she's digging it, I figure I better start thinking of ballplayers quickly. So I figure it's one out, the ninth, the Giants are up. Mays

*lines a single to right, he takes second on a wild pitch.
Now she is digging her nails into my neck... Haller singles,
Mays holds third. Now I got a first-and-third situation.
Two out, the Giants are behind one run. I don't know
whether to squeeze or steal. She's been in the shower for
ten minutes, already.*

Cycling

The true route to success is to realize that holding off
on climaxing does not have to mean maintaining your erection
non-stop. For a really wild hour in the sack, try this:

1. Let yourself get to the very brink of orgasm and then stop.

2. Engage in some non-penetrative sex play with your
partner.

3. You may well lose your erection. DO NOT PANIC. Keep
fooling around until it comes back.

4. Repeat.

5. After an hour of this, finally allow yourself to
climax. Warn your partner to stand well clear.

26. Make Your Own Sex Toys:

A little imagination goes a long way (but not too far without some means of retrieval, or you could hurt yourself).

Once you're in a horny head-space anything can become grist for your erotic mill. The ordinarily mundane world of household objects can become an erogenous wonderland of exciting possibilities.

Think Laterally

The most obvious route is to find something phallic and use it as a dildo or butt-plug (depending on size). This presumably is why God invented bananas, cucumbers, and zucchinis. But don't limit yourself to this. Spanking, pinching, stroking, tickling, and tying are all erotic techniques, so think laterally. A hair brush can be used to spank, and then turned over to scratch (be gentle though!). Clothes pegs could become nipple clamps. Sexy lingerie makes for erotic blindfolds or wrist ties.

Go Electric

There are plenty of domestic power sources you can tap into in order to supercharge your sexual thrills. A washing machine on full spin cycle could provide the motion in your ocean. Stick a zucchini on the end of an electric toothbrush and voilá—instant vibrating dildo. And never underestimate the orgasmic potency of a well-directed shower head.

Obscene Applications

Caution is advised when improvising sex toys. Emergency doctors dine out on tales of hapless patients attempting to explain how light bulbs got stuck up their butts. Don't become an ER doc's meal ticket:

- **Think twice before using anything that is larger than the orifice into which you are inserting it.**

- **Never insert anything you can lose hold of—it's important that anything penetrative should have either a wide/flared base to prevent full entry, or a means of retrieval (e.g. an attached cord).**

- **Don't use anything with rough/sharp surfaces or anything breakable.**

- **Use lubrication at all times.**

- **Be safe. Don't do anything that will cut off circulation, obstruct airways, or put you in serious danger.**

27. Cast a Sex Spell:

Back in the day, magic was a sort of technology used to manipulate secret forces in the natural and supernatural worlds in order to achieve things you couldn't manage by normal means— i.e. getting laid. In the Middle Ages, the association between magic and sex became quite hysterical thanks to the witch craze, while in modern times the revival of witchcraft and magic by the Wiccans and their ilk has also concentrated on sexuality.

Psychodrama

What this adds up to is a rich store of sex spells both ancient and modern, which you can use to attract a sexual partner, arouse them, and achieve better sex. Most important of all, however, a spell or incantation is a form of psychodrama that you can use to get into a more erotic mindset yourself. Regardless of whether you believe in magic, casting a spell really can enhance your sex life.

Gingerbread Man

An important principle of magic is the Law of Sympathy, which basically says that like influences like. An example of this is the belief that since spices like chile or ginger excited and warmed your mouth, they would have similar influence on your genitals (see Make Traditional Aphrodisiacs, page 140). Accordingly ginger was popular in sex charms, and a traditional use of the gingerbread man was in a sex spell, for use by a woman who wanted to snare a particular man. Here is how she would use it:

1. The lovesick woman undresses and lies on a bench.

2. A wooden board is placed across her genitals, and the spellcaster uses it to mix and knead the dough for a gingerbread man.

3. The spellcaster shapes the dough into the form of a man—supposed to represent the object of the sex spell.

4. While the gingerbread man is baking, the spellcaster chants at the woman an explicit description of the sex she will have with the object of the spell.

5. Meanwhile, the woman visualizes the sex and tries to increase her arousal level, eventually bringing herself to orgasm, possibly with help from the spellcaster.

6. The cooked, enchanted gingerbread man is presented to the object of the spell. Eating it ensures he will fall under its influence.

7. Even if it doesn't work, everyone involved has had a really good time, or at least a tasty cookie.

28. Tell Someone They're Crap in Bed:

If someone isn't meeting performance targets in the board-
room, they'll get a dressing
down; why should performance
shortfalls in the bedroom be
treated any differently? The
only question is how you plan to
conduct what could be the most
delicate conversation you'll ever
have. Which style suits you best?

Be Straight

"I'm sorry but I don't feel that
I'm fulfilling my sexual potential
with you."

Be Brutal

"You don't know what you're doing in bed. You don't know how
to give oral sex, how to do foreplay, how to have intercourse,
or how to make me come. You don't last long enough/you take
far too long. You make funny faces. Oh, and you need to wash
more often. I think that's all."

Be Gentle

"Baby, I think you're great and I'm sure you'll find the happiness you deserve, but sometimes couples aren't sexually compatible and I think we might be one of those couples."

Be Nasty

"Making love with you is like being groped by a dead warthog with rigor mortis which is trying to do an impression of a dead fish with rigor mortis."

Be Hugh Grant

"So, uhm, uh, listen, would you, er, no, no that's not quite—er, at least, that's not to, er, hang on, no, I mean, yes, or rather I... er, oh dear, I'm not really making much, er, well, that is..."

Be Self-deprecating

"I feel like I'm just not bringing out the best in you."

Be Euphemistic

"You're not ringing my bell. You're not floating my boat. You're not putting the mustard on my hotdog. You're not inflating my airbed. You're not rattling my carriage. You're not toasting my bagel."

Be Incomprehensible

"I just don't think we're really interfacing on a synergistic level, in terms of optimizing our satisfaction strategies for maximal mutual benefit."

29. Have Sex with the Same Person for the Rest of Your Life:

Frequency of sex naturally declines over the course of a relationship, until many long-term couples simply accept a decline to zero, and reconcile themselves to either sublimating their sexual urges altogether or finding other outlets (e.g. outside the relationship). But it doesn't have to be this way. The key words are variety and communication.

Spice of Life

If you keep doing exactly the same thing for long enough, it will eventually become stale, whether it's cooking pot roast every Sunday or doing it missionary style one Saturday every month. You need to find ways of injecting variety into your sex life, and this doesn't simply mean trying lots of different positions (although this can help—see Do 23 Positions in a One-Night Stand, page 166).

Here's how to keep it fresh:

• **Push your boundaries. Dare to venture beyond vanilla sex. Consider anal stimulation (for both him and her), sex games, bondage, and dom-sub play.**

• **Sex toys. Get some. Use them. Try out different ones.**

• **Role-play. You may feel silly/self-conscious, but role-play is highly effective at spicing up sex. Let your imagination run wild.**

Fantasy Island

With the best will in the world, you and your partner are unlikely to remain the sole and undivided fantasy object of one another's dreams. Rather than feeling threatened by this, embrace it. The imagination is the greatest tool for both variety and eroticism, and can be indispensable for extending your active sex life together. Share fantasies, talk about them, elaborate on them, act them out, role-play them—whatever it takes.

Communication is Key

Both of you will change and grow over the course of a relationship, while your libidos, sexual styles, and many other aspects of your sexual relationship will also change. The only way to cope with these is to keep communicating. For instance, introducing variety through, say, anal stimulation, could be a major problem for one partner. The only way to get around this is by talking about it.

If all this sounds like hard work, that's because it is. Lifelong sexual compatibility is not something that simply drops in your lap. You have to keep working at it, non-stop.

30. Spot the 8 Sexual Styles of Men:

The Artist: Thinks he's a sexual master. May be caught admiring his own silky moves during sex; keen on cunnilingus and foot rubs (because he thinks he's brilliant at them). Look for: silk sheets and bathrobes; casually scattered editions of the *Kama Sutra*.

The Soldier: Believes there are only three approved positions—missionary, doggy, and astride—and that technique should be the same in all three cases: bang away as hard as possible until ejaculation. Look for: white boxer shorts; keeps socks and watch on during sex.

The Hippy: Thinks that sex is "like, totally a sacrament, yeah?" Will attempt awkward positions that involve your face in his unwashed armpit. May spend time appreciating the "like, total beauty" of your genitals. Look for: incense, hair, linen trousers, lots of cushions.

The Tantric Hippy: Much more dangerous. Will insist on having sex while sitting up cross-legged. Too focused on achieving mutual multiple orgasms to actually manage an ordinary single one. Look for: yoga mats, singlets, sensual massage/aromatherapy oils, whale music.

The Metrosexual: Displays full range of sexual skills. Expects you to reciprocate. Hopes you will suggest butt plugs. Keen to cuddle after sex but really thinking about football. Look for: personal grooming products (especially hair wax), black-rimmed glasses, loft-style apartment.

The Postman: Delivers his package like he was dropping it off through a mail slot. Confuses quantity with quality. Be warned: may have several ports of call on his route. Look for: shifty demeanor, always in a hurry, very protective of his cell phone.

The Guru: Thinks he's going to teach you about "real sex." May offer to "really open you up." May in fact know some good tricks, but you can learn them all in one night. Look for: knowing references to Skene's gland, collarless shirts, has own sex toys.

The Cowboy: Wants you to ride him. May yell a lot. Likely to manhandle you and possibly tie you to bedpost. Look for: denim, mullet, funny walk.

31. Spot the 8 Sexual Styles of Women:

The Librarian: Won't emit a peep during sex, and won't tolerate any noise from you either. Likely to shush you if you emit groans or moans. Look for: sensible shoes, ridiculously tidy bedroom.

The Samaritan: Constantly asks, Is everything OK? Do you like that? Does that feel good? Too solicitous to be sexy. Look for: concerned expression, books with titles like *I'm OK, You're OK*.

The Lecturer: Believes men need detailed direction in bed. Will keep up a constant stream of instructions; may be severe if they are not obeyed. Expect post-coital feedback. Look for: bossiness, thigh-high boots, laser pointer.

The Mouse: Keeps eyes squeezed tightly shut and emits squeaks, which increase in pitch, volume, and frequency until climax. Makes ineffectual clutching movements with hands. Look for: teddy bears and other cuddly toys on bed; floral print clothes, sheets, etc.

The Gourmandise: Sexual glutton. Will demand more sex, cunnilingus, etc. Will produce alarming range of sex toys and ask you to use them on her. May suggest asking your friend to join in. Look for: hearty appetite, belly laugh, orders two puddings.

The Hygienist: Clean freak. In addition to condom will want to use diaphragm and liberal quantities of spermicide. May stop repeatedly to check that condom is intact. Will insist that you shower before and after sex. Look for: lifetime supply of condoms, STD symptom checklist taped to inside of bathroom cabinet.

The Gypsy: Free spirited and wild; potentially unhinged. Theatrically loud, especially when on top. Turned on by arguments. Look for: incredibly messy bedroom floor from sweeping everything off dressing table in order have passionate sex on it.

The Casualty: Deeply troubled but only fully reveals this in throws of sexual catharsis. Climax accompanied by wailing, gnashing of teeth and hysterical sobbing. Look for: vast library of self-help books, alarming selection of medication in bathroom, frequent references to "when I was in therapy."

32. Do a Vaginal Workout:

With the right training you can turn your vagina into a finely honed instrument of great strength and dexterity—this can boost your sexual endurance and the length and intensity of your orgasms, and your man will thank you too.

Kegel Exercises

A sling of muscles known as the pubococcygeal (PC) muscles runs from your pubic bone to your tailbone, and support all the organs of your lower abdomen, including your bladder, uterus, and lower bowel. Rings of PC muscle encircle your anus, vagina, and urethra, opening and closing them. With pelvic floor or Kegel (pronounced "key-guhl") exercises you can strengthen these muscles, improving vaginal tone and also bladder and anus control.

Suck It Up

Basically, Kegel exercises consist of tensing and tightening your PC muscles. If you are doing it properly you will feel the muscles drawing up and in. To practice, imagine you are trying to hold in intestinal gas, and tense your muscles accordingly. Now tense as if you were holding in urine. Finally, tense your vaginal muscles as if you were trying to clasp a penis.

The aim is to tighten only the PC muscles. Try to avoid tensing your buttocks, thighs, or abdomen at the same time. The most common mistake is to press down when tensing the muscles, instead of pulling up. It's worth deliberately doing it wrong so that you know what not to do. Try holding your breath and bearing down, as if you were trying to squeeze something out of your vagina. "Straining down" like this is what you are trying NOT to do.

Reach for the Stars

Persevere and you may be able to attain the fabled Vadavaka or "Mare's Trick" of the *Kama Sutra*, in which your vagina can grip a penis as if it were a hand, and then effectively masturbate it to climax without either you or your partner moving any other muscle.

33. Make Your Penis Bigger:

Most men have dreamed of achieving this since they hit puberty, and a multi-million dollar industry rests on the masculine will-to-believe that this holy grail can be attained. Here are three ways that actually work (sort of), in order of increasing risk, stupidity and inadvisability:

1. Lose weight and trim your pubes. This can make the penis look bigger, and appearance is what most of this is about. Relative size is a particular problem for obese men, and losing weight will also improve sexual stamina and performance, and could boost duration and stiffness of erections.

2. Undergo surgery to increase girth. Much more effective than length surgery (see following), this can involve silicone, treated human cadaver flesh or fat, or other tissue from the subject's own body (e.g. liposuction). Decent results are claimed for this latter material when biodegradable "scaffolds" are used. Most people are not satisfied with the results, and the surgery can be dangerous and can cause full or partial impotence.

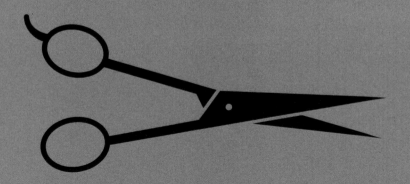

3. Try surgery to increase length. Up to a third of the erectile tissue of the penis shaft is inside the body, held in place by ligaments. Surgery to cut one of these ligaments (ligamentolysis) so that tissue "drops" out of the body cavity, can increase the apparent length of the penis. However, it also carries severe risk of damage to and dysfunction of the penis, and the vast majority of men who have it done are dissatisfied with the results.

Ways that Probably Don't Work

Methods that claim to increase penis, length by stretching/inflating the erectile tissue so that it tears and new tissue grows to repair the damage—which is effectively the rationale behind penis pumps, stretching of the penis, hanging weights on the penis and "jelqing" or "milking" of the penis (where blood is manually forced towards the head of the penis)—are of very dubious efficacy and carry significant risks of damage. There is no evidence that pills or creams work either, and many contain dangerous/contaminated ingredients.

34. Join the Mile High Club:

Anyone who has engaged in sexual activity in a craft of some sort at an altitude higher than 1 mile (5,280 feet) can plausibly claim membership of this club. Most commercial aircrafts cruise at altitudes well above this, so for most people entry to the club is gained through having sex on an airliner in mid-flight. Purists, however, claim that to join the club you need to be actually flying the airplane at the time!

Head for Great Heights

Even if this restrictive clause is waived, there is still considerable room for debate. What constitutes "sexual activity"? Is it necessary to have engaged in actual intercourse? Does the intercourse have to reach a climax for one or both of the partners? Do you have to have had an orgasm in order to join the club? Do high altitude hand- and blow-jobs count? Despite claims made on the website *www.milehighclub.com*, there is no official club and therefore no official rules.

Breaking the Law

Many obstacles lie between you and membership of this club. The biggest one is the law. Outraging public decency by having sex in a public place is illegal, while having sex on a plane in mid-flight is considered dangerous as well as breaking the law, so bear in mind that what seems like a bit of fun to you could end up in jail time, a hefty fine, and a lifelong flying ban.

Still interested? Here are your three main options:

1. Stay in your seats, but through disguise, subterfuge, and cunning use of blankets/jackets/etc., manage to engage in sexual activity without getting caught in the act. Your chances are improved if the flight is mostly empty and if it is a "night flight" (when the lights are lowered and most of the other passengers are sleeping). A promising tactic is for one partner to pretend to be sleeping with his or her head in the lap of the other. A judiciously sited blanket or jacket can then provide cover for oral sex.

2. Slip off to the toilets. This is the classic method, but it may not be that simple. People may be watching/waiting for the toilets, and beady-eyed flight attendants are likely to catch you.

3. Go on a special mile-high flight. It is possible to book a flight on a plane specifically set up to give couples the privacy to join the club in a custom-fitted cabin.

35. Back Out of an Orgy:

Group sex, tradition-
ally known as an orgy (from
the Greek orgia, a cer-
emony, ritual, or celebration
held at night by members of
secret cultic religions such
as the Dionysian or Eleusin-
ian Mysteries), has a long
and ignoble tradition. Since
Roman times the orgy has been
the epitome of sexual adven-
turousness, and in the 1960s
the new, liberated sexuality
reintroduced the idea of group
sex. Today, however, group sex
remains firmly underground,
mostly restricted to sex clubs
and private swinger parties.

Reality Bites

The truth is that some things are best left as fantasies.
While fantasizing about an orgy can be a turn on for masturbation or for sharing with a partner, the real thing is quite
a different matter. There are issues over intimacy, anxiety,
jealousy, hygiene, and sexual health. Not everyone involved
will find everyone else physically attractive. In fact, many
report that group sex parties and their participants are
seedy, un-erotic, and embarrassing.

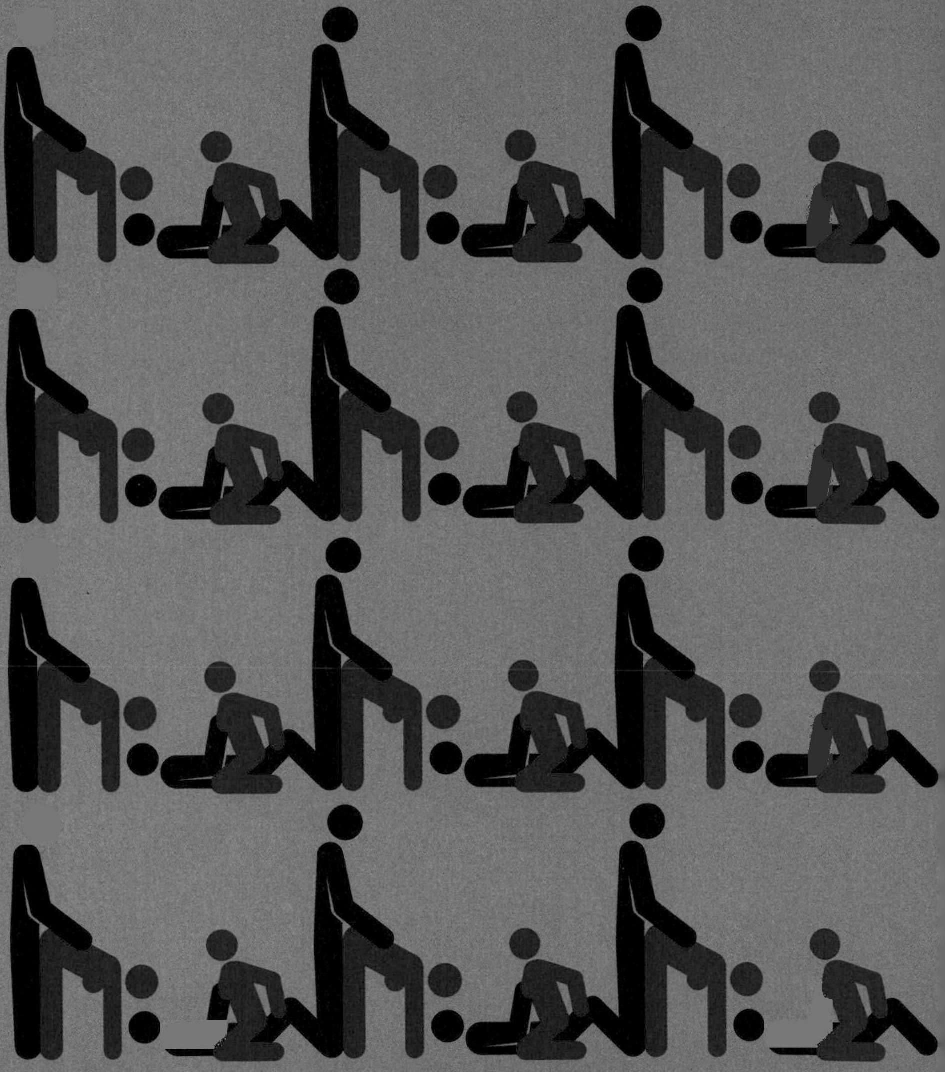

So if you're not interested in a Mongolian Cluster (a group of more than three individuals engaged in penetrative and oral sex), a Row Boat (where a woman sits on a man's penis and fellates two standing men), or a Daisy Chain (where a group sit in a circle, with each member performing oral sex on the person in front of them), what should you do?

a) **Don't accept an invitation to a group sex party.** Yes, yes, we're all curious, but think long and hard before going along. In particular, do not make the mistake of thinking that it will reinvigorate a bad relationship or be a good way to meet a partner.

b) **Make your excuses and leave.** Most group sex parties have a strict etiquette that absolutely respects your right to bow out gracefully at any point. Simply leave discreetly and there should be no problems.

c) **Scream, "You're all disgusting perverts and you make me sick you freaks!"** This is generally frowned upon, so avoid.

36. Recognize a Sex Addict:

There is considerable debate over whether sex addiction, also called sexual compulsion or compulsive sexual behavior, is a genuine psychiatric syndrome/addiction. It is not included in the *Diagnostic and Statistical Manual of Mental Disorders*, the bible of the mental health profession, but it is recognized by many other professionals and organizations. In general it is likened to other addictions, such as alcoholism, as involving compulsive behaviors that the individual cannot control or stop, and which have adverse or harmful effects.

Trouble in Mind

Some people—men in particular—might think that finding a sex addict is like hitting the jackpot, but in fact sex with a sex addict is not likely to be especially thrilling or fulfilling. Sex addicts are troubled and dysfunctional people who obsessively pursue sex because of their damaged psyches, and are likely to suffer emotional, physical, medical, financial, legal, and relationship problems as a result. Hook up with one, and you could get sucked into these problems.

What to look out for:

• The person seems to have other addictions/problems—sex addiction is often linked to alcohol, drug, and gambling problems.

• The person does not appear to actually like you or even express any interest in you.

• The person has no real interest in you.

• They try to shortcut normal small talk of an encounter in order to get straight to sex.

• Their motivation for wanting to have sex seems unclear.

• The person evidently spends a lot of time in pick-up joints.

• If male, he may have an unwholesomely extensive experience with prostitutes.

• The person may be vague or misleading about their personal situation, including existence of partner/spouse/children.

• They do not seem to derive great satisfaction from sex, even if they orgasm. In fact, they may seem depressed and/or filled with self-loathing.

• Immediately after sex the person may insist that he or she will not do this sort of thing anymore and seem distraught and depressed.

• The person may insist on very frequent sexual encounters, including at inappropriate times.

• They may push for sex in increasingly inappropriate/risky settings.

• The person is vague or unclear when questioned on their activities outside of picking up partners and having sex. This is because they don't have many.

37. Become an Erotic Film Buff:

Display your cosmopolitan credentials as a hip sophisticate by discoursing knowingly on the titillatory joys of erotic cinema—it could help you get in someone's pants!

Art vs Porn

As with erotic literature (aka erotica—see page 35), there is an important distinction between porn films and erotic films. At least this is what erotic filmmakers say. Nowhere does the controversy over art versus porn rage hotter than in the world of cinema. Follow this simple six-point plan to become an instant expert on erotic film:

1. **Watch a lot of art-house films. These often have graphic sex—sometimes even unsimulated!**

2. **Watch a lot of European films, especially very pretentious ones from the 60s and 70s. Some of these were really filthy.**

3. **Study this mini-bluffer's guide to the vocabulary of erotic film criticism:**

- Mise en scène—where the actors are fucking

- Company of players—who the actors are fucking

- Method acting—having real sex

- Wipe cut—nothing to do with cleaning up messy situations

- Character arc—not a reference to a stream of ejaculate

- Auteur—someone who can get away with filming actual fucking and still call it art

4. Do say: "trenchant commentary on modern mores," "bravura attempt to épater the latter-day bourgeoisie," "Rabelasian celebration of life," "graphic satire on the hypocrisy of prevailing ethical codes."

5. Do not say: "look at the size of his schlong," "she's going like a fucking train," "when does she get her baps out?" "I wish they'd shut up and start screwing, already!"

6. It may become necessary for you to actually watch some films. Here is a brief list of films you should claim to know about, but don't worry if you can't be bothered to sit through their entire running times—websites like Mr Skin (*www.mrskin.com*) can tell you exactly what point to fast forward to in order to get some action:

Realm of the Senses; Intimacy; Last Tango in Paris; Exotica; Dangerous Liaisons; Live Flesh; The Pillow Book; Don't Look Now; Secretary; Salò; Pandora's Box; Tom Jones; Men in Love; Lady Chatterley's Lover; Looking for Mr Goodbar; Blow Out

38. Decipher Sexual Slang:

So you've just picked up a really hot guy/gal, you're in the bedroom, and you're very turned on, when he/she turns to you and says, "How about a Rusty Trombone?" Only you don't know what this is. Should you admit your ignorance and look stupid and vanilla, or go along with it? If only you'd read this handy instant guide to deciphering sexual slang.

Going Underground

The further you venture into the wild borderlands of sexuality, the more likely you are to encounter such slang. If you don't want to look foolish, feel left out, or have a nasty surprise sprung on you, you better learn to decipher it. After all, you wouldn't want to agree to give a blumpkin, or consent to a David Copperfield, without knowing what you've got yourself into.

Basic Principles for Deciphering Sex Slang

- Think laterally: Jargon often involves a pun on what the act or organ looks like. For instance, a Double Bass is when, during standing sex from the rear, he uses one hand to play with her nipples and the other with her pussy.

- Think scatalogically: An uncomfortable proportion of sexual jargon involves anal sex or semen, and the various unpleasant combinations thereof. For instance, blumpkin refers to receiving oral sex while defecating, while a Rusty Trombone is performing oral sex on a guy's anus while masturbating his penis

- Be wary of misogyny: There's an unpleasant misogynistic streak behind much of the jargon, so ladies, if in doubt, decline whatever you've just been offered. For instance, a David Copperfield is where, while having sex from behind, just as the man is about to climax, he pulls out and spits on his partner's back to give the illusion that he's just come. When she turns around for a post-coital hug, he ejaculates onto her face.

Homework

Of course we can only scratch the surface here, so what you really need to do is engage in an ongoing research program. Study useful books like *Roger's Profanosaurus* or *Filth!*, or get online where you will discover a marvelous profusion of vulgarity.

39. Tell if Someone Wants to Have Sex with You:

Dating is such a minefield—on the one hand, you don't want to make inappropriate advances, but on the other, you don't want to miss a window of opportunity that might not be open too long.

More than Words

The first clues that your charms have penetrated his/her armor to the point where he/she may actually consider exchanging fluids with you are likely to be non-verbal.

• **Look for the signs of physiological arousal: these are bodily indicators that someone is excited, or turned on. When this happens a complex cascade of nervous and hormonal signals is released, producing physiological responses including: pupil dilation; skin flush; rapid, shallow breathing; dryness of the mouth (look for nervous licking and parting of lips).**

- Connection seeking: an interested partner is likely to seek ways of establishing more intense and intimate physical and social connection, within the restraints afforded by a public situation. Signs include: seeking and holding eye contact; leaning in (as in, they will literally incline towards you); casual touching—for example, a hand on your knee or upper arm.

- Body language: you might also see hair play (flicking, twirling or toying, especially in women); mirroring, where they mimic your postures or gestures (e.g. if you lean forward, so do they); turning towards you, or adopting a more open body posture.

Sealing the Deal

Of course these may be no more than signs of interest/flirting maneuvers. They should not be regarded as a green light. Things that really give the game away include if he/she:

- **Asks you to come up and see his/her paintings.**

- **Reveals to be wearing particularly sexy underwear—and indicates that he/she planned for you to see it.**

- **Gets naked.**

- **Shows you a wide collection of manacles, fetters, chains, or shackles.**

- **Menaces you with a dildo or similar sex toy.**

Always Ask

A note of caution: Never assume that you have correctly read signals as an "unspoken" license to proceed. You need explicit permission before moving on to sex. Plus, of course, the simplest way to tell if someone wants to have sex with you is to ask them.

40. Make All-Natural Contraceptives:

You know those occasions when you're trapped in the jungle/on a desert island, and there's just you and some beautiful sexy member of the opposite gender; it's hot and you're both sweaty, his/her clothes are artfully ragged and revealing; and there's not much to do? You'd like to be banging the grass-skirts off each other, but there's no way you want to risk an unplanned pregnancy and you can't exactly run down to the local convenience store to buy a box of condoms. What do you do? Fortunately nature offers a smorgasbord of simple solutions for the safe-sex survivalist.

Natural Contraceptives

If we extend the definition of "jungle" to, er, anywhere wild, there are several options for oral herbal contraceptives, including the wild yam (found in eastern North America), the neem plant (found in South Asia), and the pomegranate (found in dry regions around the world).

Natural Implantation Inhibitors

Again, given a loose definition of "jungle" it is possible to find plants growing wild that can be used as morning-after-pill substitutes. The wild carrot, aka Queen Anne's Lace, is found in North America, Europe, and southwest Asia. Smartweed, a relative of buckwheat, is found in temperate regions of the world. Both are great natural alternatives.

Natural Spermicides

Look for citrus trees, aloe vera plants, or beehives. Lemon, aloe, and honey are all said to have spermicidal properties (although the latter is probably a recipe for thrush). A slice of lemon placed in the vagina is a traditional—though most likely rather painful—contraceptive. Lemon juice is also claimed by some authorities to have the benefit of killing viruses, including HIV.

Make Your Own Condom

First catch a pig (or equivalent porcine animal—e.g. a tapir or a warthog might do). Kill it, gut it, extract some of its small intestine. Scrape, wash, and generally clean the crap out of it (both metaphorically and literally). Cut an appropriate length and tie off one end with a string woven from bark or bamboo fibers. Voilà, instant condom.

Natural Family Planning

Abstention is the best contraceptive. Failing that, time your intercourse to avoid her fertile periods.

Warning: Bear in mind that all of these methods have a high failure rate, and most do not protect against STDs. Also, unsupervised ingestion of herbal remedies can be dangerous.

41. Make a Love Potion:

A popular branch of sexual sorcery is the brewing of love potions. The idea is that by concocting a potion, powder, or philter and then slipping it to the object of your affections, you could make him or her fall hopelessly in love/lust with you. Famous examples of this include the legend of Tristran and Isolde, and Bottom and the Faery Queen in Shakespeare's *A Midsummer Night's Dream*.

Strange Effects

According to the wonderfully titled 1780 book *Dreams and Moles*, "To make an excellent Love Powder" you needed to:

Take nettle-feed and juniper berries, dry and beat them to powder; then burn in the fire the claw of a crab, that it may also be powdered; mix them, and giveth the party [the target] as much as will lie on a silver penny in any liquor, and it will cause strange effects without harm; by which a husband or wife [or presumably just a fuck-buddy] may be obtained.

Food Additives

The Siwans of North Africa believed that slipping your semen into a woman's food would cause her to be madly attracted to you (although this is likely to get you arrested today).

Liquor Up

Alcohol is probably the most effective love potion of them all, and inevitably featured as the main ingredient of many a witch's recipe. It is suggested that traditional liqueurs and spirits such as Advokaat, Chartreuse, Vermouth, Mezcal, and Drambuie are derived from such recipes.

The Dead Strip

Related to potions are love charms. Lady Wilde details a particularly unwholesome one in her 1890 book *Ancient, Cures, Charms, and Usages of Ireland*:

Girls have been known to go to the graveyard at night, exhume a corpse that has been nine days buried, and tear down a strip of the skin from head to foot; this they manage to tie around the leg or arm of the man they love while he sleeps, taking care to remove it before his awaking. And so long as the girl keeps this strip of skin in her possession, secretly hidden from all eyes, so long will she retain the man's love.

42. Boost Sperm Count:

Sperm count is influenced by both general health and specific nutrients and conditions. Here are ten tips for boosting your sperm count:

1. De-stress: Anxiety, stress, and depression can all lower sperm count, so if you have a stressful lifestyle or find yourself tired out at the end of every day, try de-stressing—perhaps something as simple as relaxation exercises.

2. Regulate your sexual activity: While sperm count does build up over a few days (and is reset back to a lower level by ejaculation), sperm quality degrades over time. You need to strike the right balance of "flushing out" the system and "building up reserves"—if trying to conceive, have sex/masturbate every one or two days.

3. Maintain a healthy weight: Being overweight will elevate your oestrogen (female hormone) production and lower sperm count, but being clinically underweight can lower your testosterone levels and have the same effect.

4. Testicle temperature: Optimum spermatogenesis (production of sperm) takes place at slightly lower than body temperature (this is why the testes hang free of the torso), so try to avoid tight underwear and trousers, and excessively hot environments. Take showers not baths.

5. Don't smoke: Cigarettes can lower sperm quality, while marijuana does this and lowers sperm count too.

6. Eat healthy: Zinc is the most important nutrient for spermatogenesis, so make sure your diet is not deficient. Nutritionists also recommend vitamins A, C, and E and folic acid. Best to get them from foods (like seafood, dairy, green vegetables, sunflower seeds, and broccoli respectively) rather than supplements.

7. Avoid steroids: Steroid abuse can lower sperm count to virtually zero and it can take a long time to recover.

8. Maintain sexual health: STDs can cause infertility, so always practice safe sex.

9. Avoid toxins: Some occupations may increase exposure to fertility-damaging toxins—for instance, carpenters are exposed to varnishes that can have this effect. Heavy metal exposure—which can be detected by hair analysis—has the same effect.

10. Get some sun: A healthy amount of exposure to sunlight may be linked to testosterone levels, and also regulates levels of the hormone melatonin, which affects fertility.

43. Play the Dice Game in Bed:

The dice game hails from the enormously influential 1971 novel *The Dice Man*, by Luke Reinhardt (pen name of George Cockcroft), in which a psychiatrist decides to live his life according to the roll of a die. He invents six options for what he should do next, and rolls the die to determine which one he will do. Whatever the dice tell him to do, he does, including rape, murder, and sexual experimentation.

The Music of Chance

This is where you and your bed come in. Basically the idea is to add a touch of unpredictability to your sex life by introducing the element of chance. You and your partner should agree that you will jointly come up with options for what form your sexual behavior and activities will take next, that you will roll a die or dice to decide between them, and that whatever the result, you will abide by the will of the dice.

Setting Your Options

You don't have to come up with six options every time—you could simply come up with two, and say that a roll of 1, 2, or 3 means you have to follow Option One and 4, 5, or 6 means Option Two, or you could come up with any scheme of your own (using any number of dice). If coming up with more than four options, it's probably a good idea to write them down.

Be Bold

So what sort of options should you come up with? You could stick with vanilla stuff, like "1 through 3 means we do it missionary, 4 through 6 means doggie style," but in that case why bother in the first place? Let your imagination run wild. Here's a quick list of six options to get you started:

1. She will tie you up and whip your cock with a pair of tights.

2. He will smear chocolate sauce over your nipples and clitoris and lick it off.

3. She will pretend to be frigid and incapable of arousal while you do your best to get her off.

4. He will dress up in your clothes and let you penetrate his anus.

5. She will suck you off while putting sex toys in both her anus and vagina.

6. You try to make each other come without any contact with either set of genitals.

44. Use an Egg as a Sexual Object:

You might not suspect the humble egg to have a pivotal role in the annals of passion, but the little oval can be surprisingly sexy. It is an ancient symbol of birth and fertility, while its smooth, rounded shape is sensual and tactile. Meanwhile the contents, with their close resemblance to bodily fluids, have a sexuality of their own.

Turning Japanese

It seems to be the Japanese who ran with the idea of the sexual egg the best—viz the landmark erotica of the films *Tampopo*, in which a man brings his partner to orgasm by repeatedly transferring a raw egg between their mouths; and the infamous *Ai No Corrida* (aka *Realm of the Senses*) in which a woman pops a hard-boiled egg into her vagina and then feeds it to her lover.

Eggs-cluded Activities

There are, nonetheless, many occasions where sex and eggs simply shouldn't mix. Here are ten suggestions for oviform offences to avoid:

1. Do not attempt to insert a whole (shelled) raw egg into any body orifice—the shell will likely crack and splintered egg shell can damage internal membranes.

2. Do not crack a raw egg into the vagina—apart from being unbelievably messy, this could cause yeast infections.

3. Do not crack a raw egg into the anus—eggs may carry salmonella, so you could give yourself a nasty GI infection.

4. Do not use raw egg as a lubricant—see above.

5. Do not attempt to use eggnog as an aphrodisiac—you will not get laid.

6. Never eat an egg that has been inserted into the anus.

7. Never transfer an egg from one anus to the other— again, this is a good way to transfer GI infections.

8. Do not stick a pair of eggs into your underwear to increase the apparent size of your package. You could be left with egg on your pants.

9. If you're intent on using cooked egg in your sex play, never use one without allowing it to cool down first.

10. Do not, under any circumstances, make puns along the lines of "over-eggcited," "I'm in egg-stasy," "egg-rogenous zones," *egg*cetera.

45. Have a Successful Threesome:

It might sound like the ultimate fantasy, but in reality a threesome is fraught with difficulty. How do you find participants? What etiquette should you follow? And how do you stop your erotic experiment from ruining your relationship?

Think Thrice

Before doing anything else, stop and think about whether you really ought to have a threesome. If you're in a relationship and are look-ing to invite a third person to join you and your partner, think twice and then think again. On the whole, threesomes are most likely to be suc-cessful (in the sense of not leaving at least one participant feeling upset, angry, inadequate, or anxious) when none of the participants is romantically involved with the others.

Lines of Communication

Are you or your partner bi-comfortable? How jealous do you get? Is your desire for a threesome really mutual, or is one person being pressured to fulfil the other's fantasy? Make sure you talk about all these issues, openly and frankly. Don't make the mistake of thinking that a threesome is the sexual tonic that will boost your flagging relationship/sex life.

Finding a Third

Picking up a stranger(s) for a threesome is not advisable. Ideally you want someone you know well enough to trust, and whose sexual history you have some idea about, but not well enough to risk ruining a valuable friendship/relationship. If you're part of a couple, it's important that you both genuinely agree on your choice.

Setting Ground Rules

Even though they may not sound sexy or spontaneous, ground rules are very important, or there is a risk that participants will end up doing things they don't like/will resent. Discuss which interactions are allowed, especially same-sex ones (e.g. if the threesome is MMF (two guys and a gal), are the men comfortable in engaging in homosexual activities?).

In MMF threesomes, it is important for the woman to be in control—perhaps not explicitly during sex, as this may ruin the erotic illusion, but implicitly through the use of pre-agreed boundaries for behavior, or coded safety words she can use to stop things with which she's not comfortable.

If a couple invite another woman to join them (MFF), a useful option for avoiding jealousy and hurt feelings might be to agree that only the female partner can have sex with the "invited party."

Etiquette

- If an established couple is being joined by a guest, they should go out of their way to make the guest feel comfortable. Whatever the situation, try to create a relaxed, comfortable, intimate atmosphere.

- Do not expect to leap straight into the bedroom—start with a relaxing drink, perhaps. Take it slow in both the build-up and during sex.

- In a MFF threesome the man may feel like he should be dominant, directing the action. In practice it might be better if he lets the women dictate the pace and progression, taking his cue from them.

- Don't be greedy or selfish during the actual sex. Make it your aim to ensure that the other two, especially the guest if there is one, enjoy themselves.

- It's important that no one feels neglected/shut-out, so guard against excluding one participant.

• Don't get hung up on penetration. There are many other sexual activities you can engage in. This is especially important in MFF threesomes, which may have come about because the women are bi-curious and are looking for a safe scenario in which to explore this curiosity. The man should work to enable this exploration.

Safe Sex

This is especially important in a threesome, where there is automatically a higher chance of transmission of STDs. An unplanned pregnancy in a threesome scenario carries a whole set of complications. If it results from a MMF threesome, there could be an uncomfortable "who's-the-daddy?" issue, while in a MFF involving a guest, such an event is likely to ruin a relationship if it's the guest who gets pregnant.

46. Have Mythical Sex:

Promising a potential partner "mythical sex" is a great way to lure them into bed, but what happens when you need to make good on your idle boast? Fear not, the ancient Greek gods are on hand to help you. All you have to do is follow their example.

- **Turn yourself into a bull**

When Zeus wanted to seduce Europa he transformed himself into a bull, and lured her onto his back. Once she had mounted him he leapt into the sea and swam off to an island where he had his wicked way with her.

- **Turn yourself into a swan**

Zeus adopted a different tactic for the lovely Leda, seducing her in the form of a swan. Swans are among the few birds with penises, but even so, you have to wonder if Leda wouldn't have preferred his bovine incarnation.

• Turn yourself into a golden shower

Zeus—yes, him again—took a fancy to Danae, but she was locked up in a box with only a small air hole. So he turned himself into a "shower of gold" to get in and have relations with her. Exactly what this means has been debated—a ray of light, a bunch of gold coins, or the first recorded "golden shower"?

• Get yourself a cow costume

Pasiphae, wife of King Minos of Crete, was evidently also a size-queen, for she designed a cow costume into which she could slip, in order to attract the amorous attentions of a bull.

• Work yourself into a frenzy

If you're not gifted with powers of metamorphosis and don't get your kicks from bestiality, take a page out of the book of the Maenads, the female followers of Bacchus. They would work themselves into orgiastic lesbian frenzies, during which male interlopers, such as the curious King Pentheus, would be torn limb from limb.

47. Have Satanic Sex :

The Devil has all the best moves, or so it would appear from even a perfunctory glance at the history of Satanism and witchcraft, which are littered with toe-curlingly lurid tales of lust, perversion, and highly erotic sex.

Nun Fun

Check out this fabled, fabulous account of the demonic dicking enjoyed by Sister Claire of the Ursuline convent in Loudun, France, in the 17th century, when she was "possessed" by the Devil:

She fell on the ground, blaspheming, in convulsions, lifting up her petticoats and chemise, displaying her privy parts without any shame, and uttering filthy words. Her gestures became so indecent that the audience averted its eyes [although notably they declined to intervene—perhaps they were enjoying the show too much?]. She cried out again and again, abusing herself with her hands, "Come on, then, fuck me!"

Witchy Woman

The European Witch Craze of the 15th—17th centuries saw witchcraft defined as a form of Satanism, in which men and woman sealed pacts with the Devil and his minions through perverted sex rituals. According to the 15th century *Malleus Maleficarium (Hammer of the Witches)*:

Witches have often been seen in the fields and woods, lying on their backs, and naked up to the navel. And it appears from the disposition of their sexual organs, and from the agitation of the legs, that they have been copulating with Incubus demons which are invisible to onlookers.

License to Thrill

This all sounds like lots of fun, but it seems obvious that it has little to do with actual worship of the Dark Lord and a lot more to do with the feverish, repressed sexuality of witches, the "possessed," and witch-hunters themselves. By blaming the behavior on Satan or demons, perpetrators become free to act out (or write and read about) their filthiest urges and fantasies.

You can apply the same principle through role-playing of erotic fantasies, without actually having to sell your soul to the Devil. Try out scenarios such as the lascivious witch and the repressed witch-hunter she seduces; or the nervous virginal initiate and the lecherous Satanic priest. Alternatively you could stage your own erotic Black Mass, creating an evocative theatrical setting and an atmospheric ceremony that culminates in an act of ritual sex.

48. Pretend to Be a Virgin:

There are many reasons why you might want to pretend to be a virgin, from the religious/cultural (even in contemporary Western populations there are many ethnic and religious groups that utterly prohibit sexual experimentation for girls before marriage), to role-playing, to getting into someone's pants (some people consider the "cherry" to be a great prize).

What Is a Virgin?

Precise definitions of virginity differ. The most obvious would appear to be "someone who hasn't had sex," but this opens up a new set of questions. Some people, for instance, consider that manual, oral, and/or anal sex "don't count" against virginity.

Another popular though problematic definition, which applies to women only, is that the hymen—a fold of membrane that partially covers the entrance to the vagina—is intact. In practice, however, the hymen can be congenitally so small it is hard to spot, and can easily be damaged or lost through non-sexual activity. It is also a myth that the first inter-course must tear the hymen and cause bleeding—it is, for instance, quite possible that an intact hymen is elastic enough to allow intercourse without tearing. In fact only 43 percent of women report bleeding the first time they have sex.

What to Do

• Hymenorrhaphy

The most extreme way to fake virginity is to have hymen reconstruction, a form of plastic surgery in which a flap of vaginal lining is reshaped to create a new hymen. A more short-term option, designed to meet the needs of imminent brides, is to create a short-lived flap of membrane with no blood supply of its own, but which is equipped with a gelatin capsule of fake blood.

• Simulation

For those without the inclination or resources to undergo hymenorraphy, it is possible to fake the rupture of the hymen by making entry of the penis difficult, simulating pain, and even using fake blood/self-inflicted bleeding (to spread on nuptial sheets).

• Lying

Unless your sexual partner knows previous partners of yours, he/she only has your word for your sexual history.

- **Acting Virginal**

For the purposes, of role-play it is necessary to act in a stereotypically chaste or virginal fashion. This means appearing shy and nervous; dressing appropriately (e.g. modestly, in white); blushing when sex is mentioned; and, for women, gasping with mingled appreciation/apprehension at the size and appearance of your partner's member.

49. Get in Someone's Pants by Pretending to Be Gay:

This is an old chestnut, predicated on three things:

a) Hubris: Hopefully your target is vain enough to think that he or she is so irresistibly magnetic/amazing in bed that you can be "turned."

b) Puerile fantasy: This one applies mainly to male targets—most men find the very notion of lesbians erotic, usually on the basis that somehow they will find themselves incorporated into Sapphic sex scenes.

c) False flag: Being homosexual allows you to fly under the radar and establish intimacy that might normally be precluded by suspicions of your designs.

How To Do It

1. Be convincingly gay.

For men, this may involve conforming to stereotypes, so guys—clean up your apartment, buy some decent clothes, and start grooming. Women have it easier, as you are much more likely to seduce your target by appearing to be a "lipstick lesbian"—i.e. conforming to his stereotypical fantasies of a very feminine lesbian. In both cases you have to ask yourself how far you are willing to go. For instance, would you consider kissing another guy/gal? Again, this is an easy way to get a male target turned on.

2. Establish intimacy.

Convince your target that they occupy a special place in your heart. Hopefully they will reciprocate, allowing you to establish a high degree of intimacy. As the "gay friend" you may well be allowed physical and emotional access that you would never otherwise be afforded.

3. Confide.

Now is the time to reveal your "doubts" and "confusion" over your sexuality. You never had these feelings before, but something—or someone—has awakened them.

4. Move in for the kill.

Apply liberal quantities of alcohol before administering the *coup de grace*—you never felt this way about a man/woman before, etc., you feel this real connection that goes beyond the emotional to the physical, blah-blah-blah, he/she is the only man/woman who you could ever really go for, yadda-yadda-yadda.

Warning: It is essential to be a conscience-free for this approach to work, as it involves deceit, manipulation, betrayal, and abuse of trust.

50. Get into Someone's Pants by Pretending to Be Frigid:

Everyone loves a challenge, so if you can get the object of your affections to view you as an ice king/queen who needs thawing out, you're on to a winner. Vanity will ensure that your target will not be able to resist the challenge of succeeding where all previous men/women have failed.

The Groundwork

Rent the classic Billy Wilder comedy *Some Like It Hot* and study carefully. Note how Tony Curtis, posing as a Cary Grant sound-alike playboy millionaire, successfully scores by insisting that he's "dead inside." He gets to sleep with Marilyn Monroe. What more incentive do you need?!

The Set Up

Contrive a suitable moment (after a few drinks is a good bet) and confide in your target that there's always been something missing from your life—well, your sex life. Ask them if sex is really all it's cracked up to be, and whether you're really missing out?

The Sting

After a few more drinks, develop a faraway look in your eye and tell the target with a sigh that you've always felt that the right guy/gal is out there, the one who could break the spell, lift the curse, and awake the erotic being that you just know is slumbering within you.

The Payoff

The best things about this scam are that:

a) **It's hard to get caught out. If a former boy/ girlfriend attempts to throw a wrench in the works by insisting that you were perfectly normal in bed with him/her, this is what you do: Girls—claim that you were faking it the whole time. This should shut him up. Guys—this is harder, but you could claim that you were fantasizing about someone else the whole time; or maybe that you were using anti-impotence medication, a vacuum pump, or advanced mental discipline.**

b) **Your target will feel like the cat that got the cream, which could help you to start a proper relationship (although if you wanted one of those you probably shouldn't have lied and cheated to get into his/her pants).**

51. Make Men Think You like Small Penises:

So you've finally found a great guy—he's good looking, solvent, sane, and not afraid of commitment. Even your friends and family like him. There's just one problem—his teeny weiner. You can live with it, but his insecurities are ruining your relationship. Never fear, a mixture of truth and lies should sort this out:

- **Point out that the average depth of an aroused vagina is just 4 inches, and that as a muscular, elastic organ it conforms to the dimensions of whatever is put inside it.**

- **Point out that the vast majority of nerve endings in the vagina are near the entrance.**

- **Point out that the G-spot is located just 2 inches from the entrance of the vagina.**

• Claim that you believe there is no such thing as a vaginal orgasm, that you are only interested in what happens to your clitoris, and that therefore length of cock is irrelevant.

• Ostentatiously admire Michelangelo's David and other classical depictions of men—explain that the typical Greco-Roman depiction is your aesthetic ideal.

• Point out that a small penis is better for anal sex, and that you are much more likely to let him explore "new avenues" than a guy with a huge tool.

• Claim that you have a "shallow vagina." If you want to be really extreme (or he has a *really* small penis) you could claim to have congenital vaginal atresia, a condition in which the vagina does not develop normally in utero and is shallow or absent. This could be laying it on a bit thick, however.

• Tell him that you have a particularly thick hymen with only a narrow opening, so that sex with an average/large penis would be extremely difficult and painful, whereas a small penis is just what you've been looking for.

52. Make Women Think You've Got a Huge Penis:

It doesn't seem to matter how often guys hear or read that size doesn't matter, they are still obsessed with the topic. OK, there may be a few women out there for whom a really big cock is a turn-on, but the majority of men mistakenly seem to think that this applies to all women. WAKE UP, you dumb-asses—the truth is that most women will be turned right off by the prospect of some giant member inflicting pain-

ful damage on their sensitive nether regions. Anything over 4 inches is perfectly adequate for the majority of women.

F**k It, Fake It

Still want to fool the ladies? Here are some strategies, but bear in mind that sooner or later you're going to have to display the real thing, and if there's a major mismatch between promise and product you could end up looking foolish.

• Drop hints—e.g. complain about restrictive underwear; mention the special brand of condoms that you get ("I have to get them over the Internet because pharmacies only stock normal size ones.")

• Complain that your last partner dumped you because "she couldn't handle it." When asked exactly what you mean by this, look bashful and try to change the subject. Very reluctantly allow yourself to get into the issue.

• Take the *Spinal Tap* route and hide a cucumber in your trousers. Also try socks or carefully positioned change/keys in your pockets. Of course this ploy only works up to a point, so in order to maintain the illusion you will need to stick to dry humping, which rather defeats the purpose of the whole scam.

• Penis sheath—this is a sex toy intended to recreate the effect of having a huge member. You will need some impressive sleight of hand/misdirection of attention, and a particularly dumb partner, to get away with this.

• Try some sexual positions that cause deeper penetration, which can in turn make your tool seem larger. If doing it missionary style, get her to put her feet on your chest. If she's on top, get her to tilt her pelvis and push down as hard as possible.

53. Make Traditional Aphrodisiacs:

People have been using aphrodisiacs for as long as they've been having sex. Here are some of history's greatest hits, but bear in mind that some are dangerous and/or illegal, and, with the possible exception of alcohol, none of them has actually been proven to work. Also note that something that promotes erections in the male is not necessarily an aphrodisiac for the female.

• Blood—traditionally blood was seen as a potent source of power, while blood associated in some way with virility was supposed to have particular aphrodisiac power. Try drinking the blood of a bull, a stallion, a slain gladiator, or nearest equivalent.

• Asparagus—Ok, some people find the way it makes your urine smell to be a distinct turn-off, but thanks to its phallic shape asparagus has traditionally been ascribed aphrodisiac properties. Turns out that it's also a rich source of Vitamin E, an important nutrient for genital and sexual function.

- Oysters—the oyster's aphrodisiac powers are traditionally ascribed to supposed resemblance to female genitals, but it is also a rich source of zinc, which is important for spermatogenesis.

- Yohimbe bark tea—The yohimbe is an evergreen tree from West Africa; the bark of which contains an alkaloid called yohimbine, which can help cause erections but has systemic effects and is considered quite dangerous.

- Fly agaric and mescaline—psychedelic fungus and cactus respectively, these have both been used in pre-industrial cultures as aphrodisiacs. In practice, their psychedelic effects are more likely to have the opposite effect, but they can cause enhanced awareness of bodily sensations and euphoria, which in the right context can be aphrodisiac.

- Alcohol—perhaps because of its disinhibitory effects, alcohol is probably the most common traditional aphrodisiac.

- Ginseng—the fleshy root of a plant that, because of its forked legs, is supposed to have aphrodisiac qualities. There is no consensus over whether any of the claims made for it are actually accurate.

- Spanish Fly—probably the best known traditional aphrodisiac (see page 142).

54. Make Spanish Fly:

No, this is not a how-to on to propelling inhabitants of the Iberian Peninsula through the air. It is in fact, a handy 5-step process for manufacturing your own version of the most famous aphrodisiac in history. Known as Spanish Fly because it is made from the crushed beetle of the same name, it was used in Roman times by the evil empress Livia, who would slip it into the meals of guests in the hope of provoking them into sexual indiscretions with which she could blackmail them. Later the Marquis de Sade fed Spanish Fly-laced pastilles to prostitutes.

The Spanish fly, *Cantharis* or *Lytta vesicatoria*, is an emerald green beetle rich in a toxin known as cantharidin (hence the aphrodisiac is also known as cantharides), which has an irritant effect on animal tissues and also a vasodilatory one (it causes the blood vessels to widen). The latter can help to produce erections, while the former affects the urethra, causing irritation, which the sufferer then looks to relieve through engaging in intercourse.

However, a harmful dose is very close to the active one (just 0.06g can be fatal), so administering your own is a *very bad idea*. Nevermind though, here's how to make it:

1. **Catch your beetle. Look for an iridescent emerald green beetle commonly found on olive trees and honeysuckles, amongst others.**

2. **Kill and dry the beetle.**

3. **Grind it in a pestle and mortar until you have a fine powder. It should be a yellowish or olive brown color and bitter to the taste.**

4. **The beetle contains up to 5 percent cantharidin by weight, so you need to use less than 1.2g to avoid giving a fatal dose. However, even a sub-fatal dose could still cause lasting kidney and liver damage, and harm to the bladder, urethra, and penis. So basically there is no safe dose. Like we said, don't try this at home.**

If determined to risk poisoning and death, make a tincture by soaking a miniscule amount of powder in alcohol, then dilute this tincture repeatedly to achieve a concentration of around 1 part per million. Take 1 ml of this with plenty of fluids. Now call an ambulance.

55. Ask for Sex 50 Different Ways:

As the sexperts are keen to point out, variety is the spice of sex. So, if you always request sex in the same boring old way, consider it time to mix things up. Here are 50 suggestions to get you started.

1. Wanna do the horizontal twist and shout?
2. Feel like a four-legged frolic?
3. Shall we drill for oil tonight?
4. Can I get my banana peeled?
5. Feel like coming up for a coffee?
6. Shall we shake the sheets?
7. Shall we goose and duck?
8. Want to do some interior decorating?
9. Can we pork?
10. Thirsty for some horizontal refreshment?
11. Shall we tie a love knot?
12. Can I give you a good seeing to?
13. Shall we have a bit of the other?
14. Up for some shift work?
15. Care to dance on the mattress?
16. Wanna bump bellies?
17. Feel like a shag?
18. Can I park my pink Cadillac?
19. Will you put your lingam in my yoni?
20. Feel like a quickie?

21. Want a bit of the old in-and-out?
22. Shall we go all the way?
23. Wanna screw?
24. May I have carnal knowledge of you?
25. Shall we dive in the dark?
26. Want to come in my private chamber?
27. Shall we take a trip to the land down under?
28. Wanna get carpet burns?
29. Down to do the dirty deed?
30. Can we play the game of 20 toes?
31. Shall we copulate?
32. Would you like to park in my basement?
33. Shall we do some jiggery pokery?
34. Can you fit me in today?
35. Wanna make a baby?
36. Can I give you some love juice?
37. Wanna get laid?
38. Can we create one flesh?
39. Hungry for sweet love?
40. Fancy a bit?
41. Wanna rock with me?
42. Shall I bring my tool kit round to yours?
43. Could you butter my breadstick?
44. Feel like a workout in my private gym?
45. Wanna go joy riding?
46. Shall we get jiggy?
47. Have you got a nail that needs banging in?
48. Can my snake play in your grass?
49. You want good time?
50. Can I put my lovestick in your silk cave?

56. Throw a Sex Party:

Whether you're planning to throw a fetish costume party or host an orgy, preparation is the key. Once you're all dressed up in your gimp outfit, you won't want to be dashing off to the local store for butter and razors.

Your shopping list should go something like this:

• Cocktail ingredients for "Screaming Orgasm" and "Sex on the Beach"

• Penis-shaped ice cube tray

• Whipped cream

• Erotic movies (or straightforward porn, depending on your snob level)

• Candles

• Runny honey

• Massage oil

• Lube, lube, and more lube

• Condoms

• Exotic masks

• Sex toys (as prizes)

• Individually wrapped snacks (you know—hygiene issues)

You can tell the difference between a good and bad sex party by the way people greet each other. At a good party people say hello with a kiss, a cuddle, or a grope. At a bad sex party people say, "Hello, how are you?"

To make sure that yours is a good one, try these ice-breakers:

• Put two straws in each cocktail glass—force your guests to suck cheek to cheek.

• Play "Dick in a Box." Pass around a box that contains a smaller box that contains a smaller box that contains a smaller box, etc. The smallest box should contain a strap-on. The one who ends up with the smallest box is the winner.

• Write pick-up lines and put them in a hat. Your guests must pull one out and find someone to use it on.

• Play "Name Those Pubes." Guests sketch their pubic hair style (for example, wild bush, Brazilian, Hollywood, etc.) on a piece of paper. The host then stages an exhibition of the anonymous pictures.

• Along similar lines to "Name Those Pubes," supply guests with plasticine or clay and ask them to mold their own cock or breasts.

• Have a contest to find the best spanker/spankee or the best kisser.

• Get naked—lead by example and be first.

— 57. Do Clittage:

Clittage is a fancy term for stimulating the clitoris. It was coined by the Douglass sisters, authors of *The Sex You Want: A Lover's Guide to Women's Sexual Pleasure*. The theory is that by giving the good old-fashioned clit massage a makeover and a new name, more guys will do it, more women will

come during sex, more couples will be sexually satisfied, and the world will be full of peace, love, and joy.

A Refresher Course for the Clit-Illiterate

First, the clitoris isn't just that tiny little button that peeks out from under the hood. That's just the clitoral head. The clitoris in its entirety is much bigger—4 inches long on average—and the vast majority of it is hidden inside her body. Most of the clitoris' 4 inches is taken up by the clitoral legs (imagine a wishbone) that run backward and flank her urethra and vagina.

Just like his cock, her clitoris gets hard and erect when aroused. However, unlike his cock, it doesn't stand to attention and shout its name from the rooftops. But rest assured—

it's all going on behind the scenes. And, should a guy choose to administer some clittage at the point of arousal, this should escort her straight down the road to orgasm.

The Art of Clittage

To give good clittage it helps to know your clitoral hood from your clitoral head. The hood is the bit right at the front where the labia meets (it's the equivalent of the male foreskin). The head either peeks out from the hood or shelters beneath it. Whereas the hood can be stroked and rubbed, the head can be exquisitely sensitive. Touching the head directly when she's not ready can make her squirm—and not in a good way.

If in doubt, get down there and have a look at what's where (in a hot "I want to look at you" way rather than a gyno-checkup kind of way).

Start with some slow circling of the hood—if she isn't yet wet, put some lube on your fingers to make things smooth. Try squeezing the hood between your index and middle fingers and move them up and down. Vary your touch until she responds with moans, movements, or both. When the warm-up stage is over and you've found the kind of touch she likes, keep it up.

At this stage you can touch her clitoral head directly (but keep it light). Flick or brush the pad of your index finger rapidly back and forth. Ask for feedback. If it's too intense, go back to circling the hood. Pick up the pace as she gets more aroused. Ultimately, don't stop—it's the rhythm that's gonna get her.

58. Have a Tantric Orgasm:

The short answer is: sign up for a three-year tantric sex course. During your first year you'll learn how to breathe deeply and contract your pelvic floor muscles. During the second year you'll learn how to raise sexual energy through your chakras while having sex. During the third year you'll learn how to do all three at once.

Then, if you're very lucky you may have your first tantric orgasm.

Or you may not.

How Do I Recognize a Tantric Orgasm?

Forget the usual vaginal/penile contractions and bodily convulsions of the genital orgasm. The tantric orgasm is something much more sophisticated—it's a climax of the brain.

As Tantric teacher Margot Anand says: "Most lovemaking is very dynamic. You move vigorously and you breathe hard, building up sexual passion until you explode the energy outward in a final release. In contrast, the orgasm of the brain resembles the smooth, endless gliding of a kite in the wind. You enter effortlessly into a sense of floating, as if the boundaries of your body were expanding."

Still Interested?

If you're still keen to have a tantric orgasm, get naked with your partner and follow these steps.

1) He sits cross-legged on the floor sporting a strong erection. She hops on and wraps her arms and legs around his body. She says something like: "Darling, this is the yab yum position—did you know it symbolizes sexual union and polarity?"

2) Gaze deeply into each other's eyes and breathe in synchrony. Start rocking gently against each other while imagining sexual energy rising from your genitals up to your navel. He says something like: "Darling, I can feel the energy coming up my inner flute."

3) Draw the sexual energy higher and higher through your body—all the way up to your chest, throat, and the crown of your head—until, ahhhhhhh... your brain climaxes and you experience blissful union with each other and with the entire universe.

4) If none of this is working, quit gracefully. Instead, try going at it like hammer and tongs in the doggie position.

39. Leave Gracefully After a One-Night Stand:

We've all done it. Something that seems like a good idea after a party and 20 tequilas, doesn't seem so enticing in the morning. This could apply to the fast food you ate, the insult you shouted at your boss, or the person you chose to shag senseless.

The difference between fast food, your boss, and a one-night stand, is that the one-night stand will be lying beside you when you wake up (unless you're very unlucky, in which case you could find all three). You'll need to employ all your sexual etiquette skills to get yourself the hell out of there.

Plan Your Exit

Take stock of the situation. Attempt to recall exactly what happened. Did full penetration take place or was it a simple drunken fumble? Did you use contraception? If you can't remember, swallow your embarrassment and ask your one-night stand to give you a quick overview of what you did. Respond appropriately. Try not to look sheepish, sob, appear nauseous, or horror struck.

Give your one-night stand warning that you're about to get out of bed—it's impolite to give the impression that you can't get away fast enough. Take at least three minutes to say your goodbyes. If you're really desperate, trim this to 90 seconds.

Locate the position of your clothes on the floor (and—guys—check that you're not sporting a bedraggled condom on your penis).

Exit the bed.

Keep the Conversation Going as You Get Dressed

Whatever you do, don't fall into the fatal morning-after silence. If you can, say something nice. For example:

- **That was fun.**

- **You've got nice ears.**

- **I like your mattress. It's very firm.**

If asked, explain that you had a good time but you don't want to take things any further. Never pretend you didn't hear the question, "Can I see you again?"

If necessary, humbly apologize if you've given the impression that you were on the market for more than casual sex. And don't say "I'll call you" if you're already awash with regret.

Dress briskly, but not too briskly. Trying to get your jeans on so fast you pogo around the bedroom is embarrassing for both of you.

The Final Departure

Make your departure with aplomb and grace. Don't say goodbye in a foreign language—especially not French—or make crude hand gestures. Smile through your hangover and don't run until you're absolutely sure you're out of sight.

60. Become a Sex Surrogate:

Back in the swinging 70s, men and women fell into two camps. Those going at it like rabbits with all and sundry, and those who were too nerdy, repressed, or just too plain weird-looking to get a slice of the sexual action.

To lend a helping hand to the latter group, sex surrogacy was invented. This offered the fantastic opportunity for the more inexperienced adult to get over some of their fears and hang ups about intercourse in a hands-on way with a confident, understanding, and, above all, educationally-minded therapist.

The kind therapist would show them how to have intercourse by getting them in bed and saying, "Put slot A in slot B and... ah... just a bit higher, there that's perfect... excellent work today, Mr. Smith."

And there was never any mention of the word "prostitute," so everyone was happy.

Could You Be a Sex Surrogate?

Answer the following three questions:

1)   Are you over the age of consent?

2)   Do you know your way around the body of the opposite sex?

3)   Can you say, "Now I want you to gently pulsate your tongue over my clitoris/frenulum/perineum"—without embarrassment, irony, or laughter?

If you answer "yes" to these three questions, you are qualified to be a sex surrogate. In fact, the job's yours.

Taking the Job in Hand

You'll need to be prepared to teach your clients any or all of the following skills:

• How to touch in a nice, seductive way (rather than making a brazen and frenzied swoop for the cock/clitoris of a potential lover).

• How to take nice, deep breaths before asking a potential conquest in for a coffee and a roll in the sack.

• How to avoid coming too soon (guys).

• How to come at all (women).

Warning: you may also need to wrench the virginity from 42-year-old men with spectacles, greasy skin, and lank hair. (Think computer programmer long before the job got sexy with six figure salaries.)

Advice: during surrogacy sessions you may want to burn some incense to lend proceedings an exotic Kama Sutra-type gravitas.

A Bright Future?

Nowadays, the escort business has become more mainstream and a lot of sex surrogates have been pushed out of business. You may end up getting more business if you revert to straightforward hooking.

However, if you wish to hold on to the strictly therapeutic angle of this rather niche career, then put some letters after your name and dig out the psychology certificate you got 20 years ago. And, rather than advertising yourself with ads in phonebooks, create a website. Talk about your caring and sensual nature, and include photos showing how sexy yet reassuringly parental you are.

61. Handle a Foot Fetish:

The proper name for foot fetishism is podophilia. But since people are unlikely to say, "Hi, my name's Joe, I'm a podophile" on a first date you need to be wise to the more subtle cues.

Frequent heartfelt compliments about your shoes or a fondness for foot massages may be the first signs. And if you find him/her doing any of the following you can be pretty sure you've shacked up with a podophile:

• **Rifling through your sock drawer with hand on cock/ clitoris.**

• **Offering pre-sex pedicures (especially if accompanied by a crazy-eyed look that says, "Please don't turn me down").**

• **Nibbling almonds from between your toes while moaning and writhing in ecstasy.**

Naughty Things To Do with Feet

Podophiliacs love getting footjobs. In the case of the male podophiliac, a willing partner places the soles of her feet around his shaft and moves them up and down in masturbatory fashion—it's not going to be as honed as a handjob or as slick as a blowjob, but to the podophiliac it's pure heaven. (Girls—just one tip if you're going to attempt this: cover your feet in massage oil first. It just makes the whole maneuver more pleasurable.)

A footjob for the lady podophiliac consists of a big toe being gently pushed into her vagina or several toes massaging and tickling her clitoris.

Some podophiliacs have special tastes and requests—for example, they may favor a specific color of nail polish on the toenails, they may want the toenails to be filed into a particular shape, or they may insist on the feet being clad in cotton socks that they can then lustfully peel off.

Toe-sucking is big among the podophiliac community—both giving and receiving. To master this venerated practice, pick up your lover's foot and reverentially slide your lips over each of his/her toes in turn. Go slowly all the way down the shaft of the toe and back up again swirling and whirling your tongue. Think miniature fellatio.

When Two Podophiliacs Meet...

The most blissful union for a pair of podophiliacs is the foot 69. The couple lie foot-to-mouth and then simultaneously lavish their oral attention on each other's toes. This usually leads to a hand-delivered, toe-curling orgasm.

62. Furnish a Sex Chamber:

Having sex in the bedroom is fine for many, but if you want to take sex seriously—to be a true connoisseur of the sensual arts—you'll need to dedicate an entire room of your house to sex. If this means sacrificing a kitchen or a bathroom in the pursuit of plea-sure, so be it.

Once you've got a dedicated sex chamber, it's important to furnish and decorate it with taste. Resist the temptation to go for a hard-core S&M look (black walls, chains, and intimidating hooks). Even if you're heavily into BDSM, a dungeon vibe sort of rules out having any other kind of sex. So what you need is a fairly neutral style and the following bits of furniture.

Ramp It Up

A sex ramp will elevate her pelvis during the doggie posi-tion or the missionary position so he can enter her at the perfect angle. It just makes sex easier, more precise, and, some would say, more dignified. Most ramps are simple trian-gles of foam inside a washable cover.

The Finest PVC

OK, it's not the most glamorous item but a PVC bed sheet is important. You can put it on the bed or lay it out on the floor. It will allow you to cover yourselves in oil—or any other slippery substance—and wrestle and writhe like a couple of greased-up seals. You'll also be glad to have it during any watersport-type games.

Are You Sitting Comfortably?

A chair designed for weightless sex is a must for women who like to be on top. It's a Japanese invention, and the concept is simple: she sits on two flexible bands strung between two low stainless steel frames and then impales herself on his waiting penis (he lies underneath the chair). Then she simply bounces up and down on the flexible straps—and his penis slides in and out.

Do It on the Couch

Inflatable sex couches are specifically designed to help you get into strange sex positions. They've got nice curvy shapes—tailor made to fit your own—and they include handles to hang onto if the ride gets bumpy.

For Swingers Only

If you love vertical sex, but find it difficult to maneuver, a sex swing suspended from the ceiling is essential. With her bum and back supported by straps and her feet in stirrups (optional), he can penetrate her from a variety of titillating angles and heights.

63. Sculpt Your Pubic Hair:

Sculpting your pubes is an essential sexual style statement. Without it you will never gain membership of the sexual elite, you'll be shunned at sex parties, and it's possible that no one will have consensual sex with you ever again.

If the best you can do is a casual trim down there with a pair of nail scissors, so be it. But it's better to purchase a pubic hair template and shave your pubes into a specific shape. This must be a shape that says something about your character. A pubic hair style that doesn't act as a kind of sexual resume is not worth having.

Sculpting a Masterpiece

Select your pubic template. You can buy one online, get it from a salon, or make your own. Some suggestions:

- **An arrow that points downwards (i.e., to your cock/clitoris)**
  - **A heart**
  - **An exclamation point**
  - **A lizard**
  - **A question mark**
  - **A smiley face**
  - **A flower**
  - **A skull and crossbones**

Now stick your template on your pubes and shave off any hair that isn't covered. (If you're an intrepid pube stylist, you can wax rather than shave—buy a waxing kit with templates included. Warning: it hurts.)

Once you've got your desired shape, you can sculpt and style it as you wish. Smooth the hair into points with hair gel, fluff it up with a comb, trim it, thread some beads on it, or dye it a nice bright shade of pink or orange.

Your newly depilated skin deserves attention too—draw the eye to it with some pubic stickers or crystals. They stay on for several days, even in the shower.

64. Do 23 Positions During a One-Night Stand:

If you're feeling agile and want to try—as Prince famously sang—23 positions in a one-night stand, here's one way to do it. Your mission is to move seamlessly from one position to the next.

Caution! Before you embark on the following sequence, make sure you have these by the bed: drinking water, lube, high-energy snack bars, and some erection-maintenance cream (it doesn't work, but some guys might appreciate the placebo effect). Oh, and some anti-inflammatory medication for afterwards.

1) The missionary position

Enough said.

2) Knees up

She raises her knees in the air. It's slightly sexier than having them splayed out on the bed, as per the previous position.

3) Koala hug

She wraps her arms and legs around his body. Think cute koala clinging to a branch.

4) V for victory

She unwraps her legs and raises them straight up in the air in a wide V-shape.

5) Aerobics class

She brings her legs closer to her head and he grasps her ankles.

6) Porn star

He keeps hold of her ankles but moves into an upright kneeling position and thrusts vigorously—macho porn style.

7) Break time

She rests her legs along the front of his body as he sits back on his heels.

8) Chest pump

She puts the soles of her feet on his chest. He pumps.

9) Stick insects

She puts her legs back down on the bed, feet together. He lies on top. Think two stick insects.

10) Rock n'roll

Put your arms around each other and do a 180 degree roll. The goal is for her to end up on top without breaking the penis-in-vagina seal.

11) Cowgirl

She sits up, knees on either side of his hips, and rides him cowgirl style.

12) Squat thrusts

She puts her feet flat on the bed and her hands on his chest. In a frog-like, squat she raises and lowers herself on his pole.

13) The pleasure seat

She rests her legs along the front of his body and leans leisurely back on her hands.

14) The interlude

She lowers herself so that her head rests between his feet.

15) The twist

The trickiest maneuver so far: she sits up and twists by 180 degrees on the axis of his penis. She ends up facing his feet.

16) The backward cowgirl

She leans forward, grabs his legs, and rides him.

17) The cuddle

He sits up and wraps his arms around her from behind.

18) The doggie position

Another challenging but possible maneuver: move from the cuddle into doggie (she's on all fours and he's behind).

19) Upward doggie

She kneels upright.

20) Downward doggie

She lowers her body so her chest is on the bed.

21) Point of collapse

She lies flat on her front, he lies on top of her, taking his weight on his elbows.

22) The grand finale

He moves into a push-up position and thrusts. Ideally, you both have an orgasm around now.

23) Spoons

You both roll over until you're lying on your sides in the spoons position. Now pass out.

65. Find Her A-Spot:

Just when you thought you knew your way around a lady's pleasure zones, a sexpert goes and comes up with a new one. You may be able to locate the G-spot and clitoris with the accuracy of a world weary gynecologist, but until you know where her A-spot is, your erotic repertoire will be woefully incomplete.

The new kid on the block of sexual hotspots is the A-spot. It was "discovered" by a Malaysian doctor called Dr Chua Chee Ann and he "unveiled" it at the 11th World Congress of Sexology in 1993.

Just to make things confusing, the A-spot also goes by these names:

- **The A-zone**
- **The anterior fornix**
- **The anterior fornix erogenous (AFE) zone**

Tracking It Down

Whatever you want to call it, it's deep inside her vagina on the front wall. If you know where her cervix and her G-spot are, it's about halfway between the two. You'll need to use your fingers to access it—it's not one of those areas that gets a natural penile massage during intercourse.

The A-spot is a nerve-rich area that makes her go weak with pleasure when it's pressed and stroked (maybe even sending her on a fast-track to orgasm when combined with clitoral stimulation).

A-spot stimulation is also a fast way to make her wet (try it when you're trying to penetrate her in a toilet cubicle and there's a long line outside). In fact, Dr. Chua Chee Ann highly recommends a strong dose of A-spot attention for women who suffer from vaginal dryness.

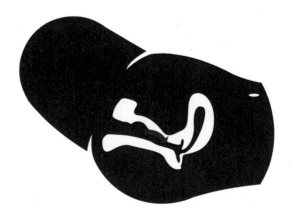

What To Do When You Find It

As well as discovering the A-spot, Dr. Chua Chee Ann also devised a way of touching it—which he snappily named the AFE Zone Stimulation technique.

Fortunately, the AFEZS technique is really easy to do. You simply slide your finger(s) along the front wall of her vagina—stroke/press the upper wall with the pad(s) of your fingertips until the whole area feels slick and wet.

Now move your fingertip down to the lower front wall of her vagina, where her G-spot is. Now back up again. Now back down again.

Continue this in-out stroking movement applying pressure as you do so—but ask her for feedback about what feels best.

Afterwards, give yourself a pat on the back and demand a P-spot massage in return. If she says, "what the f**k's that?" politely direct her to page 16.

66. Fist for the First Time:

Fisting—the art of inserting your whole hand into a lover's anus or vagina—is not for the faint hearted, the virginal or the large handed. First-time fisting requires a lot of communication and patience, plus a vat of good quality lube. Because fisting puts the recipient in a vulnerable position, it's best to try it in the context of an established, trusting relationship rather than casually throwing it into the mix on a one-night stand.

Prepare to Make Your Entrance

Apply plenty of lube to your chosen orifice and announce your presence with a finger stroking and circling the entrance.

When things are heating up, assume your positions. If you're working with a vagina, the woman's best position is on her back with her knees wide apart and you sitting between her legs. If you're working with an anus, your fistee will be most accessible to you in a doggie position.

Going In

Despite its name, one you thing you definitely can't do is go in with a clenched fist. Instead, start by inserting your index or middle finger (or both) and then add your thumb. Make your hand into the shape of a duckbill and softly insert it into the vagina or anus. Pace: extremely slow.

As your hand makes its upward journey, let your remaining fingers join the duckbill. Add more lube to minimize friction. And communicate. Fistees—a simple "mmmm" will let your partner know you're not being split in two. Fisters—the occasional "more?" or "OK?" will reassure your lover you've got their best interests at heart.

When your fingers are fully immersed, you can start to curl your hand into a fist.

Final Destination

Once you've gone as far as you dare—and remember there's no shame in going knuckle-deep rather than wrist-deep—keep your hand still and share a quiet moment with your partner. The stimulation of fisting comes from the feeling of extreme fullness, so, fisters, don't feel like you need to do any fancy finger moves. Fistees, if you're in danger of tensing up, breathe deeply with long exhalations.

67. Cure Priapism:

The response of many men to a case of priapism would be, "Hey, why cure this?"

Priapism is a medical condition in which the penis stays erect for many hours. The blood flow to the penis is disrupted, leaving you with a monumental stiffy that just won't go away.

Despite it's obvious attractions, priapism doesn't offer an opportunity to give the sexual performance of your lifetime. This is because it really hurts. And if you don't act fast to get your willy back into a state of diminutive limpness, you risk scarring and future impotence.

If you suspect you're suffering from priapism, don't bother with self-help treatments. This isn't something that can be cured with an aspirin, a homeopathic remedy, or a cup of hot herbal tea.

Doctor, Doctor—I've Got a Rod of Steel

Get straight to your nearest ER and expose your priapic monster to the first medical professional you come across. Beg them to do any of the following:

- **Give you a decongestant drug that will reduce blood flow to your penis.**

- **Inject your penis with your drugs that make the veins narrow.**

- **Insert a needle in your penis and syringe some of the blood out.**

- **Insert a shunt (a passageway) into your penis that will divert the blood flow.**

- **Pack your penis and perineum in ice.**

- **Tie off any leaking arteries that may be causing the problem.**

For Greek Myth Lovers

Priapism is named after the Greek god of fertility Priapus. He sported a penis that was huge and eternally erect. He was also considered grotesquely ugly and his image was frequently used as a scarecrow.

68. Realize You're a Porn Addict:

When is too much internet porn *too* much? How do you know when you've Googled one MILF too many? Is it the blisters on your fingertips/genitals?

Is it the way you giggle when your friend/wife/sister announces they're "going for a facial"? Or is it the fact that you now view any pubic hair—beyond the skinniest of landing strips—as freakish?

According to psychologists, a porn addiction is "a compulsive behavior that persists despite serious negative consequences for personal, social, or occupational function."

In other words, you could be on the verge of losing your spouse, your friends, and your job, but searching for words like "gang bang," "blowjob," and "hot, horny young lesbians at frotting party" seem somehow more pressing.

– Addiction Checklist –

If the following sound familiar to you, it could be time to log on to *www.pornaholicsanonymous.com*:

• You spend hours at a time searching for online porn. You stay up all night looking for the perfect bit of "natural" footage. You quit only when you're too tired to see the screen, or your genitals have been so thoroughly thrashed they can't take any more.

• After an Internet porn session you feel guilt/remorse/self-criticism. As one Internet porn addict said: "It was the pit of hell. I got no satisfaction, but I went there anyway."

• You don't feel you can control your behavior. Maybe you've tried to stop but the lure is too strong. Maybe you've got a credit card that's dedicated to your porn payments.

• Looking at porn has a negative impact on your day-to-day life and relationships. You'd rather go to bed with your laptop than with your lover. Your boss is looking askance at the stains on your trousers and the crazed look in your eye.

• You're spending more and more time on the Internet and you need increasingly hard-core or specialist porn to get aroused.

• You look at Internet porn when you're stressed/angry/lonely/depressed. It's a distraction or an escape. Hours online can feel like minutes. You haven't seen daylight for 24 hours. You think it's time for dinner, but it's actually 6am.

69. Seduce Someone on the Phone:

When attempting a phone seduction your approach must be carefully tailored to the level of intimacy you've already achieved with the seductee.

If it's a long-term lover, you can say pretty much any-thing you like in the name of seduction. In fact, your best bet is to just pick up the phone and get on with it.

If it's someone you barely know, a soft approach is essential. Care and caution are advisable.

Start Tepid and Get Warmer

When attempting to seduce by phone, you don't want to give the impression that flirtation is your sole intention. Your aim as the call progresses is to give the sense that you are gradually being overcome by your interlocutor's voice—or their incredibly interesting conversation.

To this end, don't begin the telephone call by growling or purring through the phone. Speak in the same voice you'd use for a close friend of the same sex—intimate, but not too intimate; warm without being salacious (yet).

Follow the usual rules of flirtation: listen to what your seductee is saying and find a way of empathizing or agreeing. Ask questions to show how fascinated you are—even if the subject is about plumbing, tax, or headlice. If he/she says anything remotely funny, cackle with ready laughter. Have some jokes or quips on hand (making your seductee laugh is one of your most powerful weapons). But don't desperately shoehorn in a joke if the mood is sincere rather than frivolous.

Pay compliments, but don't preface them with the words "Has anyone ever told you...?" (You'll sound like a bad movie script.) Instead offer simple, snappy charm. "You've got a cute voice" will do nicely.

If things are going well, consider consolidating your gains by ending the phone call and following it up with another one later.

However, if things are going *very* well and you're in a reciprocal flirting situation, try some dramatic statements. If they fall flat, claim you were just teasing. Try one of these:

- I'm in love with your voice.

- You're fantastic. Can we pretend we're on a phone date?

- I know it's a cliché, but you sound so sexy.

- You sound like a voiceover artist—you don't do erotic phone calls do you?

- You're so interesting to talk to—I feel like I already know you.

- I wish we could meet.

70. Be a Good Sub:

In the kinky world of BDSM the word "sub" refers to the submissive partner in a sexual power game. Your first step to being a good sub is to find a good dom (meaning "dominant partner"; see page 13). Trying to be submissive when you're masturbating alone in your bedroom doesn't have the same kick as surrendering to a real-life, whip-bearing lover.

Get the Mindset

Having found yourself a dom you need to tune your brain to a new frequency. Stop thinking of yourself as a mature, dignified adult with a respectable day job and a set of rights. Instead think of yourself as a naked and humble servant, willing to be humiliated at all times. As a good sub, your function is to obey and surrender.

Of course it helps if all this gives you a gratifying sense of freedom and turns you on in the process (otherwise there's no obvious point to the exercise).

Your Wardrobe

What should you wear as a sub? The correct answer to this question is "whatever your dom wants you to wear." Be prepared to put on anything that demeans or renders you powerless in some way. This might include a blindfold, a dog collar (with leash), or handcuffs. Be prepared to have your hands tied behind your back or—in more intense BDSM encounters—your wrists bound to your ankles behind your back.

Act the Part

If your dom tells you to crawl across the floor on your hands and knees, whip them with a peacock feather, or deliver an hour of analingus, you must do precisely that. And with an air of obsequiousness and gratitude. Your only escape route through all of this is to utter a "safeword." This is a word that you both agree upon beforehand—it's a quick way of communicating, "No way am I doing that—let's call it a day and have a cuddle in bed."

— 71. Do Analingus:

It's a dirty job but someone's got to do it. Polishing the chocolate starfish (that's licking the anus to the uninitiated) isn't everyone's idea of fun.

First, there's the risk of swallowing some rather unpleasant germs. Second, there's the, er, taste. Third, there's the delicate matter of access.

Fortunately, these problems are often overcome by alcohol... many people are introduced to analingus while drunk.

A few tequilas can make bottom-kissing a far more palatable idea than it would be normally. It can take on a risqué aura in its sheer boundary-breaking naughtiness.

Alternatively, the gentleman of the couple may make a simple slip of the tongue when attending to the lady's front bottom. Whichever route you take to get there, you may find that once you've started, the moans and groans of your ecstatic lover mean there's no way back.

The Sober Analinguist

If you prefer a less impetuous and, let's face it, a safer and tastier approach to analingus, you'd be well advised to spend some time on preparation.

If you are the giver of analingus, your best bet is to be candid and ask your partner to sanitize their backdoor before you make your approach. (Alternatively, invite him/her to have a bath/shower with you and casually offer an "erotic soaping.")

If you're to be the receiver of analingus, be kind and give yourself a thorough cleansing. It doesn't have to be an enema with surgical spirit, but it does have to be a comprehensive soap and hot water job. And proceed to the bedroom immediately after washing.

For the very well prepared a dental damn will protect you against all health and flavor issues. Try to avoid cheap substitutes, such as plastic wrap and empty BBQ-flavored chip packets.

Get in Position

Once you're cleansed—and possibly damned—it's time to assume positions.

1)   **The yogic option: lie on your back and put your feet behind your head.**

2)   **The exhibitionist option: get on all fours with your ass in the air.**

3)   **The coy option: lie on your back with your legs wide apart and your bum raised on a couple of pillows.**

⎼ Now What the Hell Do I Do? ⎼

Well... just lick. It's not big and it's not clever, but it is comparatively easy. The anus responds well to both clockwise and counterclockwise movements. It loves both a flat lapping tongue and a pointed flicking tongue. And a little shallow penetration can be especially thrilling for the recipient. It is particularly suitable as a first course to anal sex and before you know it ATM (ass-to-mouth) will be a regular part of your evening.

72. Look Cool While Stripping— for Guys:

Brave is the man who offers to strip for his lover. Whereas the inexperienced lady stripper can take refuge in some strategically placed candles, an expensive pair of stockings, and a pair of high heels, the gentleman has fewer options.

Slipping your trousers oh-so-slowly over your butt and thighs while looking coy and pouty just won't cut it if you're a dude. Not even if you've got a gym-honed body.

Women strippers have another advantage: men make eager and forgiving audiences. Whereas men love to ogle, women just aren't as visually motivated. In fact, a woman presented with a stripping lover may be likely to giggle or, worse, snort with derision.

The Odds Are Against You, But...

You can look cool while getting your kit off.

Your most important tool (no, not your penis) is attitude. As long as you present yourself as confident, careless, and, importantly, ironic, the clothes you wear and the moves you make don't matter so much.

Having said that, peeling off sweaty gym clothes while flicking your hips like a self-styled Chippendale isn't going to impress anyone—you will need some form of "routine."

The safest stripping outfit is a suit and a tie and your sexiest undies. (By the way, this means sexiest undies for you—tight pants only look good on tight bodies.)

Once You're All Dressed Up, You're Ready to Go

1) Do a quick attitude check. Think: casual and careless with an insouciant twinkle in your eye.

2) Use one hand to unbutton the jacket and then shrug it off.

3) Use one hand to loosen your tie. Keep your head still. Maintain eye contact with your lover. Not the vacant "I can stare you out" eye contact, but the sexy "wait until I get my hands on you" kind. Now unbutton your shirt (keep looking at her—not at the buttons), shrug it off and drop it on the floor.

4) In a swift action, unbutton and unzip your trousers. Don't linger or fumble (and definitely don't stop for a quick grope of yourself). And keep your junk covered—a flash of testicle doesn't have the aphrodisiac effect on a woman that you might hope for. Having said this, the shape of your erection outlined by your pants can provide a tantalizing promise of things to come.

5) Kick off your shoes, then slide your trousers down your legs quickly, and hook your thumbs into your socks as you go. Get the whole lot off in one efficient swoop.

6) Don't stand around looking lame in your pants. Pounce. Give her the job of removing the final item.

Three Stripping No-Nos

1) Never fold a discarded item of clothing. And definitely never put it on a hanger. Once it's off, act like you don't care whether you ever see it again. Worrying that your favorite shirt will get creased or dirty on the floor doesn't create the necessary impression of abandon, urgency, and torrid impatience.

2) Pace and timing are important. Don't aim to get your kit off at breakneck speed—you'll not only look desperate, you'll also risk falling over. Don't go too slow either— you don't want to look tentative or nervous.

3) Don't run your hands seductively over your nipples, hips, or bum—leave that stuff to the girls.

73. Do a Standing 69:

More scientifically known as "mutual oral sex in a vertical position," the standing 69 is one of those sex acts that can go either way. It can be a stunning piece of sexual performance art or a dangerous debacle that leads to the break-up of your relationship. It works best if he's got muscles of steel and she's as light as a feather. Growing up in a circus helps too.

Here's How You Do It

1) She lies on her back on a bed with her head hanging off the edge.

2) He approaches the bed and stands with his legs on either side of her ears.

3) He leans over her and wraps his arms tightly around her waist.

4) She wraps her arms and legs around him.

5) He stands up again—this time with her attached.

6) You secure oral-to-genital contact as soon as possible.

Tip: get your tongues moving quickly. This isn't a position in which you'll want to hang around.

Pros and Cons of the Standing 69

- The sheer challenge of getting into the position teaches you teamwork and cooperation in tricky situations. Scaling Everest will be nothing after this.

- You can smugly congratulate each other for pulling off such a tricky stunt.

- If you're ever asked, "What's the stupidest position you've had oral sex in?" You'll be ready with an answer.

- If he drops her, she risks head injuries and a trip to the ER.

- If she senses she's falling off, she may hang on to him in the only way she can—with her teeth.

- If you're even slightly mismatched in mouth-to-genital alignment, you'll be tonguing each other's navels.

The Cheat's Version

Install a metal bar in your bedroom. Position it so that when she hangs upside-down from it (knees hooked over the bar) and he stands on the ground, you've got perfect mouth-to-genitals alignment. This is also known as the "acrobat's version."

74. Tie Someone Up During Sex:

The very first thing you need when tying someone up is not top quality rope, bondage tape, or leather handcuffs—it's consent. Once you've secured this, then you can go shopping for the kinky stuff, safe in the knowledge you won't be facing a lawsuit.

Despite what women's magazine articles may say, silk scarves are not the best tools for tying up a lover—not only do scarves cut into the skin, they can also be difficult to undo in a hurry. The same goes for any kind of string or thin rope or cord. Your best bet for kinky restraint is one of the following.

Bondage Rope

Pop online and get yourself a measure of rope from *www. kinkyropes.com*. Synthetic fibers are best—they're not only easy to loosen, they're also comfortable, smooth on the skin, and fully washable. Choose a fairly thick rope—at least 3/8 in diameter—that won't cut off circulation. To learn how to tie a bondage-style knot, get yourself a copy of the *Erotic Bondage Handbook* by Jay Wiseman.

Bondage Tape

If you're a bondage novice—or you just never bothered to learn how to tie a knot properly—bondage tape is ideal. Unlike normal packing tape, which sticks to hair and skin (and gives your lover an involuntary waxing), bondage tape sticks only to itself. It's made of brightly colored PVC that you simply cut to length and wrap around your lovers wrists or ankles. And you're done—no knots, no fuss.

Bondage Cuffs

Even easier than bondage tape. You don't even have to get a pair of scissors out—you just whack the cuffs on the nearest pair of willing wrists or ankles. Don't use anything with a lock on it—the consequences of losing the key are too great. Velcro or buckles are so much safer.

75. Give a Kinky Blowjob:

Take pride in your work. Create some dramatic tension by stroking him through his pants first. Nuzzle him through the fabric with your mouth. Slowly ease him free with your hands and, rather than going straight for the kill, tease him with your lips, tongue, and graze him softly with your teeth.

Hand and Mouth

Your hand and mouth are a winning combo in the world of oral sex. Not many men will turn down the mixture of a soft, wet, and yielding touch with a harder more directed touch. Use your mouth to form one ring and your fingers and thumb to form another. He'll also appreciate a hand up top while you're down below licking his balls.

Make Him into a Voyeur

Let him see the action. If you've got long hair, throw it back so he can see your face. You may think oral sex makes you look like a hamster with mumps. He, however, will not. In his eyes you're a sex goddess.

Position is important in affording him the best view. Kneel between his legs and look him in the eye as you run your tongue up and down his shaft. Let him see the porn-style details—the flick of your tongue on his glans or the thread of pre-cum as you pull away. Another position that rates high in terms of kink is straddling his chest with your back to his face and then going down. This gives him access to all areas from anus to clitoris—it's just one stop short of a 69.

Alternatively, introduce an extra touch of voyeurism with a full-length mirror. Get him to stand in profile, then kneel in front of him and take him in your mouth. This way he gets to see both his cock and your face—he'll feel like the one-man audience of a dirty movie.

Climax Scene

If you want to up the kink-factor, don't spit discretely into a tissue after he comes. Instead hold him in your mouth and make him feel like you're drinking him (which you are). Alternatively, let him come on your body—kinkiest hotspots are your face, neck, or breasts, or all three at once.

76. Play "Seduce the Bottle":

This is a sexy party game with a twist. Participants are led to believe that the game involves seducing a wine bottle. So far, so embarrassing. Then after guests have humiliated themselves by, for example, kissing the neck of the bottle, licking its rim, or trying to penetrate it, the true nature of the game is revealed.

The only tool you need for this game is a wine bottle— drink the contents first.

Preparation

Ask your guests to sit on the floor in a circle. Tell them that you are about to pass round an empty wine bottle. As each player receives it he or she must describe and then perform a sexual or seductive act they would do if the bottle was the most sexy man/woman they could imagine. Explain that acts can be mildly seductive to downright filthy. To stretch players' imaginations, no one is allowed to repeat an act that has already been performed by another player.

Stage One—The Easy Part

The host starts off with the bottle. He or she describes and performs the first act. A tame example might be massaging the bottle's "shoulders." A risqué example might be fellating the neck.

Then the bottle is passed to the player on the left. When everyone in the circle has performed a sexual act on the bottle, the host describes stage two of the game.

Stage Two—The Saucy Part

The host explains that each player must now repeat the act that was previously performed on the bottle on the player to his/her left. The game ends when it comes full circle and the host receives the final act of seduction.

Explain to players that if anyone refuses to carry out their chosen act, they face a sexual forfeit.

77. Indulge a Pygophiliac:

A pygophiliac needs to see or touch a pair of buttocks in order to become aroused. Pyge = buttocks; philia = love. If you find yourself in bed with a pygophiliac, here are ten things to make their night.

1) Stick little bits of chocolate on your naked butt cheeks using maple syrup or honey as glue. Offer yourself as a sweet snack to your lover.

2) Make your lover watch as you stand in the shower and drizzle massage oil over each shoulder so it runs sloooowly down your back and over your bottom. After a tantalizing wait, ask him/her to come and rub the oil in.

3) Invite your lover to make a plaster cast of your bum.

4) Use your ass as a massage tool.

5) Undress your lover in your best seductive style and then strip yourself. Stand back to back and rub, rock, and roll your buttocks against his/hers. Think of it like rubbing noses.

6) Guys: go to bed wearing nothing but a pair of chaps. If you haven't got any, cut the ass out of your Levi's. Gals: wear a short skirt with nothing on underneath. Now stand in front of him while he's watching TV. Bend over very slowly. When your bum is high in the air, teasingly lift your skirt up to reveal your ass.

7) Drench yourself in oil and lie on your front on a PVC sheet. Instruct your lover to slither their way up along your body starting at your feet and stopping when you are cheek to cheek.

8) Ladies: introduce him to the concept of the butt wank. He slips his penis in between your heavily lubricated buttocks and slides up and down. (No anal entry required.)

9) Write "lick here" on your bottom. (Tip: if it's difficult, cheat with a Post It note.)

10) Dance like Shakira. Naked.

78. Be an Ethical Slut:

If you want to have sex with multiple partners but you don't want the hassle of lying about it or being labeled a whore, there's a simple answer. Re-brand and re-market yourself as an ethical slut (aka a polyamorist). Tell your friends and lovers that monogamous relationships are no longer "you." Declare such relationships to be repressive and outmoded. Present yourself as a brave pioneer of an alternative lifestyle.

• **Have sex with anyone you want. On the condition that you do it with honesty, openness, and integrity.**

• Know the philosophy of ethical sluttery inside out so that you can explain yourself when challenged. Read *The Ethical Slut: A Guide to Infinite Sexual Possibilities* by Dossie Easton and Catherine A. Liszt.

• Practice what you preach. When your girlfriend/ boyfriend follows you down the polyamorous road, don't start getting possessive.

• If you're explaining yourself to your parents, don't use the word "slut." Say, "I'm practicing consensual non-monogamy."

• Learn the lingo. Your "primary" is the person with whom you are most intimate with/spend most time. Your "secondary" is the next person down the ladder. But be aware that some polyamorists believe this sort of hierarchical labeling is negative. Instead they might refer to lovers as their "intimate network." "Polyfidelitous" means having sex only with a defined group of people.

• Wear a parrot badge to identify yourself to other subculture members. "Poly" is the informal name for both polyamorists and parrots.

• Be prepared to spend a lot of time negotiating ground rules with sexual partners, particularly if you live with/are married to one of them.

• Be prepared to spend an even longer amount of time discussing why you or your lover are feeling jealous. Talk endlessly about how you can "work towards resolving your ownership and control issues."

— 79. Deep Throat:

Girls: deep throat is like learning to apply a condom— it should first be practiced in solitude on a cucumber. That way, when you're with a partner and the spotlight's on you, you'll be able to perform with professional ease.

For the aspiring deep throater, the main challenge is to overcome that pesky little gag reflex at the back of the throat. Take a cucumber of reasonable size and slide it slowly into your mouth. When it hits your throat, instead of going "urgggruuuhhhhhgg" and throwing up, sit sedately and tell yourself that it's just a case of mind over matter. Breathe deeply through your nose—just like you do in yoga. Don't picture yourself puking. If you know how to meditate, now's the time.

Once you've conditioned your throat to relax in the presence of a phallic vegetable, it's time to put your skills to the test on a real live penis. Choose either of these positions.

Position One—The Head Hang

Girls—lie on your back with your head hanging off the edge. Open your mouth.

Guys—arrange yourself so that your dick is level with her mouth. This will probably mean kneeling on the floor using pillows to adjust your height. Push your penis into her mouth and slowly down her throat. "Slowly" is the key word.

Girls—put your hands on his thighs to show him how fast he can move in and out.

Position Two—The Straddle

Girls—sit astride his chest (bum almost in his face) and lean forward. Take his erection in your mouth and slowly down your throat—once you've got him comfortably inserted, move your head up and down—at your own pace.

Guys—no sudden thrusts.

— 80. Spot "The Clap":

What happens if, while gazing lovingly at your lover's genitals (or even your own), you notice something "wrong"? It could be a lump, a bump, a swelling, or a red patch—how do you know if it's something "normal" or something that should send you rushing to the clinic?

A Strange New Discharge

Treat any new and unusual secretions from the vagina or penis as suspicious. A green-yellow discharge may be a sign of gonorrhea or chlamydia. In women, a thick white vaginal discharge can mean thrush and a watery grey one can mean bacterial vaginosis (neither are technically STDs, but, hey, you still need to treat them).

Sores and Blisters

If you spot a genital blister, a sore, or anything that's weeping, oozing, crusting, or scabbing over—take action, see a doctor. Painless genital ulcers or sores may signal the first phase of syphilis. Tingling, painful genital blisters may be a sign of herpes.

Bumps, Bugs, and Growths

Unusual bumps and growths (not those caused ingrown hairs) need professional diagnosis. Small or large growths, either alone or in clusters, could be a sign of genital warts. Red-brown bumps could be a sign of scabies. And you can be pretty sure that if you see tiny insects clinging to your pubes, you've got a case of crabs (aka pubic lice).

Invisible STDs

Even if you or your lover are sporting a pristine set of genitals, this doesn't rule out an STD. Some STDs such as genital warts have an incubation period (meaning they're brewing below the surface and will take a while to appear). Others, such as chlamydia, may be symptomless, so you don't know you've got them until you get tested. If in doubt, go and get checked out.

Don't Rely on Sight Alone

Sometimes an STD can be felt rather than seen—if you or your lover have burning sensations while peeing, pain during sex, or tenderness in your abdomen or genitals, you know the drill...

81. Advertise for Sex:

What used to be restricted to the personals section in the newspaper has now exploded into a massive Internet phenomenon. Millions of people routinely advertise for everything from lifelong platonic relationships to instant, disposable sex. If you're reading this you're probably tending more to the latter category.

Learn the Language

Personals have their own bizarre and frankly irritating jargon of acronyms and abbreviations. Familiarize yourself with them or face the consequences. The last thing you want is to confuse BHM with BHOF or TDTM with TSWC. And if someone tells you TWHAB, you need to be prepared. (See box for dictionary of terms.)

No Time Wasters

Don't waste your time or that of respondents by pretending. Be direct in the advert and you'll save yourself and everyone else a lot of trouble. After all, you don't want to be a

CWOT do you? But be aware that the sort of people who answer adverts for sex aren't necessarily the sort of people you dreamed of having sex with.

Fine Line

When describing yourself in a personal ad, it's important to be honest so that people don't think you're a liar as soon as they lay eyes on you, but positive enough not to scare people off. Are you a SNAG? Can you pull off VGL? Probably best to avoid NIFOC, and be aware that if you put VFM people might think you're a prostitute. Never put false stuff in your ad—lies of omission are fine.

Aim for Mars or Venus

Remember that men and women get hot for different things. Men want to hear that women are tactile, sexy and wild. Women want sensual, loyal, and honest.

Put Yourself in Their Shoes

People will read between the lines when they look at your advert. You say "adventurous"; they read "slept with hundreds of people." You say "open-minded"; they read "desperate." You say "free spirit"; they read "substance abuser." You say "HWP"; they read "cuboid." Craft your advert accordingly.

Dictionary

BHM: Big Handsome Man

BHOF: Bald Headed Old Fart

CWOT: Complete Waste Of Time

HWP: Height Weight Proportional

NIFOC: Nude In Front Of The Computer

SNAG: Sensitive New Age Guy

TDTM: Talk Dirty To Me

TSWC: Tell Someone Who Cares

TWHAB: This Won't Hurt A Bit

VFM: Value For Money

VGL: Very Good Looking

82. Give Earth-Shattering Cunnilingus:

For too many men the vagina is an uncharted area, marked on the male mental map with the forbidding legend "Here be dragons!" Men may protest that "she doesn't like me to go down south," but that's probably just an indication that they don't know what they're doing. If you want to cross the line from average in bed to truly sensational in the sack, you need to become a black belt at cunnilingus.

Lesson One: Mental State

Great cunnilingus is in the mind—hers, not yours. In order for a woman properly to enjoy oral sex she needs to be relaxed and at ease. Women are sensitive about how they look, taste, and smell, on top of which she may suspect you don't really want to be down there. You need to be utterly convincing; make her believe that cunnilingus is your favorite thing in the world, that you're desperate to give it, that it's more for you than for her, that you're loving every second of it, that you treasure the sight, smell and taste of her.

Lesson Two: Conditioning

Tongue exercises build dexterity and endurance. Practice this routine until your tongue is fighting fit: Move the tip of your tongue up and down. Move it from side to side. Thrust it forward repeatedly. Increase the pace until failure. Rest and start again.

Lesson Three: Positioning

Your head needs to be squarely between and slightly below her thighs so that you can apply upward strokes of the tongue against the underside of her clitoris. You mainly want to be coming at the clitoris from underneath.

Lesson Four: Build Up

Begin with continual upward strokes of the tongue, in a lapping fashion. Move on to feather light twirling of the tongue on top of the clitoris itself. Try occasionally inserting the tip of your tongue into the vagina.

Lesson Five: Finish Her!

Concentrate once again on the clitoris. Use your fingers to stretch the labia sideways to help get the clitoris standing proud. Try stimulating one side and then the other, but always from underneath. Note that one side is often more sensitive and erogenous than the other. Learn to process her verbal and physical feedback to direct your strokes most effectively.

83. Have Sex in Crowded Places:

There are several reasons why you might want to have sex in a crowded place, and how you go about it depends on exactly what your motivation is. Which of the following best describes your reasons for wanting to make public what normally stays private?

A. Exhibitionism—according to the "bible" of psychiatry, known as DSM-IV, this is "sexual gratification, above and beyond the sexual act itself, that is achieved by risky public sexual activity and/or bodily exposure," including "engaging in sex where one may possibly be seen in the act, or caught in the act."

B. Frotteurism—intentional rubbing up against someone for the purposes of sexual gratification, often achieved by being in a crowded place such as a packed subway car. Amusingly, this is defined in the official diagnostic manual as a "courtship disorder."

C. Ochlophilia—this is the technical term for sexual arousal as a result of being in a crowd (from the Greek ochlo, meaning mob or crowd).

Assuming that it's (A) that floats your boat, here are five tips for success:

1. Get a good lawyer. Having sex in public, or deliberately going for it somewhere you know people are likely to see you, is illegal in most places (in fact in some places it could be fatal!).

2. Be discreet. Presumably you'd rather not need Tip 1, so try to cover up your doing it. Blankets, big overcoats, and billowing dresses can screen your fumblings from the world. Also try to position yourselves strategically behind bushes, high seat backs, etc—use whatever cover is available.

3. Timing is everything. Choose your moment—e.g. if you're on an airplane or a coach, wait until everyone else is asleep.

4. Dress smart. Deck yourselves out in easy access clothing, such as short skirts, crotchless knickers, button-fly boxers, etc. This way you don't have to drop your trousers around your ankles to achieve congress.

5. Look innocent. Assuming that you followed Tip 2, and you're not buck-naked with your legs akimbo and someone's arm buried up to the elbow in one of your orifices, you might plausibly just be having a cuddle or resting your head in/sitting on your partner's lap. Joe Public or Jane Attendant will want to believe it, so try to look beatific.

84. Find Your Inner Sexual Animal:

Native Americans believe that each of us has a spirit guide in the form of an animal, a creature that represents our inner selves, and which can guide us to greater wisdom and personal development if we can get in touch with it. It stands to reason, therefore, that each of us also has an inner sexual beast, and if we can make contact, this animal inside could guide us to greater sexual fulfillment.

Below are described the six sexual spirit animal guides, as handed down by the timeless wisdom of the ancients. In order to determine which best describes you, meditate on the following descriptions, if possible in an altered state of consciousness. One of these creatures should appear to you.

- **Beaver: Industrious and hard working in the bedroom, the beaver is tireless in its efforts to ensure that its partner is satisfied. The beaver finds fulfillment in teamwork (group sex) and complex constructions (DIY sex toys).**

- Snake: Potent but slippery, the snake can penetrate to the heart of its partner's desires, but can also be selfish and capricious. The snake finds fulfillment in dark burrows (anal sex) and encircling its prey (bondage).

- Cock: Arrogant, brash, and boastful, the cock is proud of its sexual prowess and not afraid to crow about it. The cock finds fulfillment in strutting its stuff (lap dancing) and being highly vocal (loud sex).

- Pussy: By turns prowling and cuddly, sly and affectionate, the pussy is mercuric and unpredictable, but also graceful and elegant. The pussy finds fulfillment in toying with its prey (sex games and domination) and being stroked (masturbation).

- Ass: Strong, stoic, and patient, the ass can bear tremendous burdens and has great powers of endurance. The ass finds fulfillment in being worked hard (marathon sex sessions), whipped into shape (masochism, submission), and chewing the cud (oral sex).

- Tit: Nervous, flighty, and alert, the tit prefers not to linger and is always on the lookout for the next thrill. The tit finds fulfillment in inventing ways to get cream (creative oral sex), nesting (furnishing a sex gym), birdsong (vocal sex), and pecking (erotic biting).

85. Live Without Sex:

Sex. Uh! What it is good for? Absolutely nothing!

Sex is the source of many of the world's ills. Over-population, unwanted pregnancy, sexually transmitted disease, cervical cancer, abuse, emotional pain, broken promises, sticky sheets, guilt, lies, jealousy, and betrayal—the list goes on.

All over the world millions of people voluntarily remain celibate—a good deal more are "incel," or involuntarily celibate. Such luminaries as Newton, Tesla, William Pitt the Younger, Immanuel Kant, and, er, Cliff Richard, were celibate (the first four never had sex in their entire lives!).

As celibacy advocates like to point out: SEX IS NOT COMPULSORY.

Accentuate the Positive

Giving up sex is a bit like giving up smoking. Step one is to free yourself of the mindset that says you are "giving up" something. Look upon your celibacy as gaining something.

Celibacy allows you to devote all the mental and physical energy you usually expend on thinking about, seeking, and dealing with the aftermath of sex, on more rewarding things like work, creativity, spirituality, and gardening. You can look at others as people in their own right, not as potential sex objects. You can free yourself from a world of negative emotions.

A Whole New World

Don't be defined by your sexuality (or lack thereof). The whole point about being successfully celibate is that it allows you to rise above the often sordid world of sex, and expand into a new world of infinite possibilities (except the possibility of getting laid).

Own Your Decision

Educate yourself about the true cost of sex. Don't be celibate because you have to be, do it because you want to (unless you're celibate because no one will have sex with you, in which case you're screwed, metaphorically speaking only).

Don't Forget Your Five-Fingered Friend

Proper celibates don't masturbate because they are trying to free themselves from the bonds of desire, but if you're not prepared to go 100 percent Brahmacharya (the Hindu practice of right living, which includes total celibacy), try being your own best friend instead. Who needs men/women?

86. Lap Dance like a Professional:

Forget *Showgirls*—lap dancing is not about dry humping a guy until he comes. Exquisite lap dancing is a state of mind—yours first, his later. You can only give a truly erotic performance if you feel sexually charged and empowered. And remember that a lap dance is more about the journey than the destination.

1. Feel good about yourself. You can't dance sexy if you don't feel sexy. Get in the best shape possible and use makeup, hair, and wardrobe to make yourself feel good. Don't worry about what he might like, only think about what makes you feel hot.

2. Choose an outfit that lets you move easily, but more importantly one that makes you feel sexy.

3. Pick music that turns you on rather than worrying what he might like.

4. Find your inner lap dancer—adopt a persona and role-play it to the max. You are no longer a mild mannered office worker/mother-of-two. You're now a heartless, heart-breaking vamp who toys with men.

5. Get him to sit in an armchair with armrests. Make sure it's sturdy enough for you to work around.

6. Take control. In a lap dance you are the sexual predator, he is the prey. You have the power, he is your pawn. Don't just think this—believe it, know it, and show it.

7. Maintain eye contact.

8. Don't let him touch you. You can touch him, but he is to remain passive and helpless. Make sure he understands this rule from the start.

9. Use your hair as an erotic implement. Run your fingers through it, pile it up, let it cascade down, even whip him with it.

10. Don't get naked too soon; don't grind or dry hump too soon. Tease him and work up to a climax when you are ready.

87. Get in the Mood When You're Not in the Mood:

Sexual arousal cannot be turned on and off like a light. Libido is the product of a complex set of factors, from age and fitness to genetically determined testosterone levels and stress. Contrary to the stereotype this is not primarily a female issue—both sexes are affected by influences that act to counter arousal. Sometimes this is OK. A loving partner should be able to understand that you are not in the mood and not make a big deal out of it. But there will be occasions when it would really help if you could overcome your lack of arousal. Here are three tips for manufacturing the mood for love.

Relaxation

One of the biggest dampeners on libido is stress. It's hard to feel turned on when you're anxious or on edge, with distracting thoughts intruding. You need to relax and minimize negative or intrusive thoughts. Simple relaxation or even meditation techniques can help to achieve this. Try a five-minute relaxation exercise: sit in a comfortable chair, focus on your breathing, and systematically tense and then relax each muscle group in your body. Once you've done this, you can move on to one of the other strategies.

Visualization

The imagination is a powerful tool. Give yourself a few moments to focus intensively on a visualization and you might surprise yourself. Choose a fantasy, or simply a setting in which you feel both relaxed and erotic. Picture it in your mind's eye, paying close attention to specific details. Use all of your senses to explore the visualization.

Act "As If"

It has been shown that a powerful tool for achieving desired outcomes is to act "as if" you have already achieved them. This effectively means role-playing the mood you wish to experience. Think about how you feel and—more importantly—act when you are in the mood. Perhaps you verbalize your arousal—try saying the same things. Mimic the physical components of arousal—breathe more quickly, part and lick your lips, swallow nervously, caress yourself, open your eyes wide, flick your hair... whatever it takes.

88. Eat Your Way to Stronger Orgasms:

Some people are capable of having "food orgasms," where their enjoyment of a particular food or meal is so intense that it actually triggers an orgasm. The scene from *When Harry Met Sally*, where Meg Ryan fakes a comically loud climax while enjoying a pastrami sandwich, may spring to mind, but true food orgasms are usually much more subtle and quiet. Sushi and spicy foods like wasabi or curry seem to be good triggers, but presumably a true gourmet can get off on any sufficiently good food.

Come to the Table

But can diet have a significant impact on the orgasmic potential of non-foodophiliacs? Problems achieving orgasm are overwhelmingly more common in women, so they are the focus of most of the research and advice, and according to Maryon Stewart, author and founder of the Women's Nutritional Advisory Service, "In one recent study, we found 69 percent of the women we saw got their libido back relatively quickly with a healthy diet, supplements and an exercise regime."

Oil Boom

These are the three pillars of the orgasm-boosting regime laid out by Marrena Lindberg, in her book *The Orgasmic Diet: Boost Your Libido and Boost Orgasm*. She particularly emphasizes the need to:

a) **boost levels in the brain of the neurotransmitter dopamine by taking large daily doses of the essential fatty acids found in fish oil, specifically EPA and DHA supplements, and eating two squares of dark chocolate a day**

b) **reduce serotonin levels by avoiding coffee, cigarettes, and starchy/sugary foods**

c) **boost testosterone by eating a low-fat, low-carb, high-protein diet and taking zinc and magnesium supplements.**

Will It Work?

Lindberg's recommendations may well work, but perhaps not for the arguably simplistic neurochemical rationale she offers. No one disagrees that being fitter, healthier, and thinner will boost your libido and possibly your orgasmic potential, but this is probably as much to do with enhanced self-image and the positive psychological consequences as it is with your diet.

89. Prepare for a Dirty Weekend:

Your weekend away may turn out to be Destination Disappointment if you don't put some effort into preparation.

1. Don't leave it until the last minute

Romance, attraction, arousal, excitement—these things don't happen all on their own or take care of themselves (especially for ladies). Start planning and preparing weeks or even months in advance.

2. Get fit

The single best thing you can do is get in shape. The better you feel about yourself, the sexier and hornier you will become. Plus your partner is more likely to respond. A dirty weekend is a good motivator for a new diet and exercise program, and the anticipation of showing off a sexy new you is the ultimate thrill.

3. Abstain from penetration

Prefixing your weekend away with a week or fortnight of sex games in which you follow a strict no-penetration rule will ramp up your libidos to fever pitch. The sexual tension will be crackling as you check in.

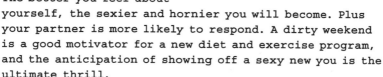

4. Pamper yourself

Invert the usual routine by indulging in spa/tanning saloon time before you go away, not during. This way you'll be groomed to perfection and feeling great about yourself from the moment you tumble into your bedroom.

5. Set the scene

Guys—recognize that romance is arousing for girls. It may seem corny or kitsch, but build up to the weekend by leaving little notes and treats for your partner during the week. Call ahead to arrange for a gift to be waiting for her when you arrive—tastefully sexy lingerie under the pillow may prove to be a worthwhile investment.

6. Get down and dirty

Girls—recognize that for guys the thrill of the dirty weekend is embodied by the first part of the phrase. Make him feel like you're back at the start of your relationship, when there was more raunch than romance.

90. Have Fantastic Sex Without a Partner:

"Sex is a beautiful thing between two people... between five, it's fantastic!" said Woody Allen, but what did he know? In the immortal words of Fleetwood Mac, "You can go your own way." There are manifold methods for the mono-sexual to achieve maximum self-sat-isfaction. Some are dealt with elsewhere in the book—see "Perform Auto-Fellatio" (page 23), "Be Creative with a Rabbit" (page 236), and others.

Even Better Than the Real Thing

If the five-fingered shuffle isn't doing it for you, explore the wild world of sex toys (or if low on funds, try making your own—see page 70). Of particular interest might be the highly realistic sex dolls that you can now buy. Extremely lifelike, they are better looking and in better shape than most real partners, and they're always ready to party.

Get Creative

Spice up your onanistic operations by using a partner substitute. Men: pillows, pies (see the movie *American Pie*), fruit (e.g. a watermelon with a hole cut out). Women: cucumbers, shower nozzles, fruit.

Mind's Eye

The real key to solitary satisfaction, however, is to enrich your fantasy life. The power of your imagination can give you experiences and encounters more fulfilling and erotic than any in the real world. Follow these steps to improve your powers of visualization:

1. Choose a quiet, relaxing environment, like a bathtub full of scented water or a big, comfy bed, where you can focus and not be distracted. You need to minimize the sensory input from the outside world in order to maximize your immersion in your internal one.

2. Be as specific and detailed as possible with your visualization. If you are imagining yourself in a room, what color are the curtains, what scent are the candles giving off, what sound do the leather thongs make as you tighten them?

3. Use all five senses. Don't just think about what you're seeing, imagine textures and tastes, scents and sounds.

— 91. Be a Candaulist:

According to legend, 8th century BCE King Candaules of Lydia (in modern-day Turkey) wanted to prove to his chief minister Gyges how beautiful his wife was, and plotted to sneak him into her chamber while she was undressing. Gyges got an eyeful but she spotted him and confronted him with a choice—her honor had been outraged, so either he or her husband must die. Needless to say, Gyges was the next king of Lydia.

Three's Company

From this legend derives the term *candaulism*, which refers to sexual arousal/gratification derived from watching two other people (one of them usually your partner) have sex. Traditionally a man would watch his wife get serviced by another guy. This can be appealing for a number of reasons. Older men who cannot perform themselves can get off by proxy. Long term couples looking to spice up their sex lives can engage in it as a form of swinging. It can be a form of emotional sadomasochism, in which the woman "tortures" her husband by cuckolding him right before his eyes.

Some candaulists have special cupboards or closets built to facilitate their vice, so that they can observe other men with their wives without the guest knowing what is going on. In Belle Epoque France, it was apparently a popular practice for men to take their wives to a brothel to watch raunchy stage shows, after which the women would be encouraged to have sex with another man. At many swinging parties, watching partners with others is more popular than actually participating in sex.

Candaulism for Beginners

If you want to try this with your partner the most important thing is consent. For a woman to get over her ingrained resistance to the practice it may be necessary to role-play a non-consensual, "surprise" intrusion, but doing this for real is a violation and not advised. In general, follow the guidelines for a threesome (see page 119) and be aware of the potential for similar pitfalls and dangers.

92. Give the Perfect Kiss:

Since ancient times sex manuals have attempted to teach this basic art of love. The *Kama Sutra*, for instance, is full of weird and slightly useless advice: "When her lover is off

his guard or asleep, a woman should get hold of his lower lip, and hold it in her teeth, so that it should not slip away, and then she should laugh, make a loud noise, deride him, dance about, and say whatever she likes in a joking way, moving her eyebrows and rolling her eyes." Mmm, thanks Vatsayana, that should work out well.

Because we believe in being different, we thought we'd tell you exactly what *not* to do:

1. Eat as much garlic and smoked fish as possible. A raw clove of garlic is a good idea.

2. Do not use chapstick or any other form of lip protection. The rougher and more chapped and blistered your lips are, the better. Ideally you will have at least one open cold sore too.

3. Lick all around your mouth so that the whole area is wet before you start sucking face.

4. Make sure to keep your eyes open at all times. It helps if you can get a really intense stare going, but try to keep a "dead" look in your eyes. Imagine that you are a sociopathic killer who regards other humans as insignificant insects.

5. If your partner tilts his/her head make sure you tilt yours in the same direction so that you are still directly facing each other. If he/she tries to tilt back the other way, match the movement. Keep doing this as often as necessary.

6. Lurch in with your forehead at the last moment so that you bang heads with your partner.

7. Open your mouth as wide as possible and stick your tongue out.

8. Mash your open mouth against your partner's and lick all around the mouth area. Try to get saliva up into the nose if possible, and definitely onto the chin.

9. Burp violently. This works best if you can bring up some garlic/fish-scented air from your stomach to give the burp some flavor.

10. Stick your tongue as far down your partner's throat as possible. Move it around as if mimicking the actions of a washing machine.

11. Groan loudly, in a strangled, inarticulate fashion.

12. Finish off the kiss by pulling away and gagging/retching.

90. Use a Penis Pump:

A penis pump is a device that creates a vacuum around the outside of the penis in order to draw blood into it so that it becomes engorged and erect. Although they are widely advertised as tools for increasing the length and girth of the penis, there is absolutely no evidence that they can achieve this, while they do carry significant risks of causing pain/damage to the penis. The only proven effective use of a penis pump is as a treatment for erectile dysfunction, although some people derive sexual pleasure from the action of the pump, such as the American judge accused in 2006 of having used one to pleasure himself while sitting presiding over trials including the murder of a toddler!

The following steps apply to most penis pumps, but be aware that each device is different and may operate differently or have its own idiosyncrasies, so ALWAYS READ THE INSTRUCTIONS!

1. To operate, the pump must create an airtight seal around the penis, which means it must make full, clean contact with the flesh around the base of the penis. This may require trimming or shaving of the pubic hair.

2. Fit the tube over the end of the penis and press it up against the body.

3. Many models now come with built-in automatic pumps, but older ones may have manually operated pumps. Use either to create a vacuum around the penis.

4. Once the penis is engorged with blood, slip a tension ring over the pumping device and around the base of the penis shaft. A tension ring squeezes off the blood vessels at the base of the penis to retain the blood that is already in it.

5. Remove the tube and use your erection, which should last long enough to have sex. Do not leave the tension ring on for more than 30 minutes. Also be aware that tension rings can impede ejaculation.

WARNING: Do not overpump the pump or you could damage your penis, causing burst blood vessels. You may experience numbness, pain, bruising, coldness, or petechiae (spots caused by tiny haemorrhages).

94. Be Creative with a Rabbit:

The Rabbit vibrator is the best known and best selling sex toy of all time. Its popularity can primarily be traced to its appearance in an episode of *Sex and the City* in 1998.

The name derives from the rabbit-like "ears" of the clitoral stimulator that project from the base of the main shaft. Many different models from many different manufacturers are now available, including miniature ones, extra-long ones, waterproof ones and even glow-in-the-dark ones.

In fact the Rabbit is now so widespread and commonplace that it has ceased to be the daringly lascivious gadget it once was. With a bit of imagination, however, your Rabbit could become much more than a mere vibrator.

Sex Games

• Take your Rabbit to pastures new—for both him and her! Those cute little ears can stimulate the anus just as well as the clitoris. Just make sure you practice good genital hygiene (i.e. once you've applied part of the vibrator to the anus never use it anywhere else without washing it first).

• A Rabbit is such a potent tool that it makes an ideal focus for bondage/BDSM sex games. Tie up and blind fold your partner and then "threaten" him/her with the throbbing monster—quivering anticipation guaranteed.

• If your man is unconvinced of the attractions of this sex toy, apply it to his shaft and balls while sucking the top of his penis.

• Or you might consider adapting a strap-on rig so that a Rabbit can be fixed in place of the usual dildo.

• If you're feeling really creative, make the Rabbit the centerpiece of a lewd pagan erotic ritual, as a totem or idol.

Bachelorette Parties

What says "bachelorette" better than a Rabbit? But don't restrict yourself to giggles and knowing looks—make the Rabbit an integral part of the bachelorette party. It can be used as an exotic/erotic drinks stirrer, or adapted for use in silly games. Try dipping the tips of both the main shaft and the rabbit ears in ink and then getting the bachelor-ette to draw on two sheets of paper simultaneously. Make tiny costumes for its various heads and—voila!—instant animated finger puppet show.

95. Be a Sex Pest:

Are you the sort of lowlife who doesn't care about other people's feelings, or refuses to respect boundaries and propriety? Too much of a loser to get a girl/boyfriend? Incapable of connecting with real people in a genuine fashion?

Then you could be a perfect candidate to join the ever-growing ranks of the depraved, degenerate, perverted and pathetic—you could be a sex pest! Our five-step plan tells you everything you need to know to join the least desirable club in the universe:

1. **Make yourself as unattractive and creepy looking as possible. This enhances the gross-out effect you are looking for, and ensures that you are correctly perceived as a grotesquely inadequate bottom feeder** attempting to project your own deep-seated self-loathing onto others.

2. Practice your delivery of obnoxious comments. If you approach a young woman on the subway and say, "Hey, nice beasts, er, I mean breasts, yes, breasts... you have nice ones... I'm going to go now," she will laugh at you. Rehearse, rehearse and then rehearse some more.

3. Consider specializing in one of the many sub-categories of sex pestilence. Perhaps you could be a frotteur (see page 211) or very vocally food orgasmic (see page 221).

4. Keep up to date with new technology. Cutting edge sex pests are out there now using camera phones to take pictures up women's skirts. Steal a march on them by familiarizing yourself with the latest webcam or mobile blogging technology. Get yourself featured on hollabacknyc.com or one of its many sister sites, and you could be a famous sex pest.

5. Be an equal opportunities sex pest. Women can be sex pests too. Did you know that four out of five male workers have experienced harassment from a female colleague, according to a study for employment law firm Peninsula?

96. Admit to Having an STD:

Being afraid to tell your partner you've got an STD is a very natural emotion—few things are more likely to kill a passionate moment than mentioning that you have genital warts. But you have a responsibility to discuss this issue with your partner, and it's best to do it a) before you have sex for the first time; and b) before you get too involved:

1. Educate yourself. Many types of STDs are treatable and/or curable. Others may not have serious consequences, or may only be a problem some of the time (for instance, genital herpes can never be got rid of, but most people will rarely, if ever, show symptoms or be seriously infectious). In most cases transmission can be prevented through safe sex and other precautions. This is all information you need to pass on to your partner, so it is important that you know it yourself.

2. Be prepared. Know what you want to say and make sure you know your facts. Have some information/literature on

hand, such as a pamphlet or printed-out webpage, which you can give your partner. These can be educational and reassuring, lending authority to your own reassurances.

3. Rehearse with a trusted friend. Try role-playing both sides of the discussion, and don't be afraid to get your friend to act unreasonable or difficult.

4. Pick a time and a place where you feel safe and comfortable, and won't be interrupted. Some people like to tell their partners during a quiet dinner or a walk in the park, so that he or she has a chance to go home and think things through.

5. Be confident about your motives. Sharing this information with a partner is the only way to move forward with your relationship with trust and full knowledge of each other. If your partner is going to reject you, perhaps you're better off not being in a relationship with him/her.

6. Expect a happy outcome. Psychologists tell us that people more often react the way you expect them to, so go into the discussion assuming that your partner will ultimately understand and accept you.

97. Be a Sex Bore:

Have you done it in every position known to man or beast? Have you accumulated so many notches that your bedpost has been whittled down to a matchstick? Do you dismiss talk of marathon sex-sessions, threesomes, orgies, strap-on sex toys, hardcore S&M, contortionist sex and extreme genital piercings by taking a long drag on your cigarette, exhaling in a bohemian fashion, and saying "been there, done that" with an airy wave of your silk gloves? Then you sir/madam, are ideally positioned to be a sex bore.

- **Top every story told by anyone else, ever, even if Warren Beatty is regaling you with the tale of the time he was shipwrecked with a cruise ship full of Playboy bunnies on a tropical island entirely made of KY jelly.**

- **Never, ever look impressed by anyone else's sexual anecdotes, even if he or she is claiming to have had a threesome with Ghandi and a killer whale.**

- **If someone else does make a far-fetched claim concerning sexual exploits, defend them**

by insisting that, "not only does that sound perfectly plausible, I can assure that it's not as uncomfortable as it sounds."

• Feign total apathy to even the most attractive prospective partner: "once you've had as much experience as I have, you begin to realize that there's an indefinable alchemy to great sex which transcends the merely physical."

• Drop cryptic allusions to past glories—"that reminds me of Venice in '83—you'd be amazed what those gondoliers keep under their straw hats"—but always refuse to expand on them—"you'd have to have been there yourself to understand."

• Affect an air of amused indulgence towards any account of sexual exploits proffered by others.

• Memorize lists of obscure paraphilias; claim to have indulged in all of them.

• Every time anyone mentions any name at all, from Ambrose to Zelda, give a wry, citizen-of-the-world chuckle, as if fondly recalling your crazy sexploits with someone of that name.

98. Make Pain Erotic:

Traditionally the simplest way to achieve this aim was to spend your formative years boarding at a British public school, where a fevered nexus of pubertal hormones, closely confined single sex environment, repressed homosexuality and corporal punishment combined to produce deeply ingrained patterns of masochistic sexuality. The derivation of pleasure from pain—specifically flagellation (whipping or caning)—has long been known as le vice anglais as a result.

Sadomasochism in History

In fact, sadomasochism has a long and dishonorable history. The art, poetry and literature of ancient Greece and Rome bear testament to diverse sadomasochistic practices, while the *Kama Sutra* advises the use of scratching, biting and slapping as methods to enhance arousal. Flagellation became an important part of many religions, especially Christianity, and although it was primarily intended as a form of spiritual purification there may have been erotic motivations for some

participants. By the 17th century it was widely recognized that some people derived pleasure from dispensing or receiving pain.

Why Is Pain Pleasurable?

There are lots of theories, many focusing on psychological complexes formed in childhood, but there is a physiological basis. Any stimulation of erogenous zones can activate pleasure receptors, especially when you are already aroused. Something that would normally be painful can become erotic in these circumstances. Also pain stimulates production of endorphins, naturally produced opiates that produce a sort of high.

Safe, Sane, and Consensual

Sophisticated communities have grown up around erotic pain, such as the BDSM scene. Key elements for such communities are tightly controlled parameters; codes of conduct summed up by the phrase "safe, sane and consensual"; and "safe" words that the passive, "bottom" partner uses to control the action.

Beginners should start slowly. In Shakespeare's *Anthony and Cleopatra the Egyptian Queen* talks of the "lover's pinch, which hurts and is desired"—and this is a good place to start. When you are both highly aroused, try pinching the erogenous zones. Do it softly at first and be guided by your partner. Nipples are the best place to begin.

99. Choose the Best Vibrator:

Vibrators come in an unbelievable profusion of styles, shapes, functions and materials. For the uninitiated choosing one can be daunting. Plus they can be expensive, so you want to get it right first time.

Buzz or Hum?

Factors to consider initially are:

• **Power source.** Electric ones (i.e. ones that plug into the mains) are more powerful and won't run out of power at inconvenient moments, but they are less portable, can only be used where there is a power outlet, and will have cables attached. Battery-operated ones are self-contained and more portable but less powerful, plus you will have to replace the batteries periodically. Rechargeable vibrators bridge the two classes.

• **Volume levels.** How discreet do you need to be? Battery-operated vibrators tend to be louder.

• Material. Vibrators can be made of plastic, jelly, latex, silicone, glass or a simulated skin substance such as Cyberskin™. Personal preference is all important here, but bear in mind that the material you choose affects your cleaning and lubrication options (e.g. jelly vibrators are harder to clean, while silicone ones cannot be used with silicone-based lubes).

– Good Vibrations –

There are several basic types of vibrator—each is generally available in different material/power source options. Which of these styles best suits your needs?

• Traditional/basic: A straight, smooth shaft, usually in plastic or other hard material.

• G-spot stimulator: Curved so that it can be inserted into the vagina and apply pressure to the front wall, supposed location of the G-spot.

• Clitoral only: Generally small because it is not for insertion. Can take many forms, such as rabbit ears or butterfly-shaped devices that strap around hips or thigh so that they are hands-free

• Eggs or bullets: Small, pebble-like vibrators that are very portable, elegant and discreet (some do not remotely resemble a sex toy and can be carried in a handbag without fear of embarrassment).

• Combination: Dildo-like shaft with clitoral stimulator attached to base—e.g. the world-famous "Rabbit" (see page 236).

• Anal: Generally slighter; with flared base or retrieval cord to ensure they can't get away from you.

• Remote control: For inventive sex fun (see page 27).

• Balls and beads: For anal and vaginal insertion—similar but smaller than eggs/bullets (see page 252).

• Realistic: With synthetic skin alternatives now available there are some ultra-lifelike vibrators on the market.

• Waterproof: So you can take it in the bath or shower. Also easier to clean.

100. Use Anal Beads:

Anal beads are small balls that are either strung together or sit along a central stalk. The string or stalk should have a handle at the end, because one of the cardinal rules of any kind of ass play is that you have to be careful not to lose anything in the rectum, which can be surprisingly easy to do.

To Bead or Not to Bead?

The rationale behind anal beads is that the anus is packed full of sensitive nerve endings, and these get their biggest kick of sensation when opening and closing around something (just think back to your last really satisfying bowel movement). A string of beads going in or coming out gives a series of jolts of pleasure. Connoisseurs advise timing the extraction of the beads so that you pull them out at the moment of orgasm, helping to turn an ordinary climax into an amazing one.

Shaft!

Traditionally beads were of hard plastic, metal or other substance, and were on a string, but strings are impossible to sterilize properly and can easily break. Nowadays the usual form is a series of beads along a shaft, all made of silicone, jelly or plastic. Often the beads increase in size from the tip to the base of the shaft.

Slip 'N' Slide

When using anal beads obey all the rules of anal play. Use lots of lube, go slowly, communicate with your partner at all times, stop if there is pain or blood and stay clean. Do not swap or transfer sex toys from the ass to any other area, if possible cover the toy in a condom, and clean and if possible sterilize it after use. Try applying a small vibrator the end of a bead shaft—the vibrations will travel up into your ass.

101. Recognize an Asphyxiophiliac:

Asphyxiophilia goes by many names—autoerotic asphyxiation, scarfing, kotzwarraism and breath control play. It refers to the paraphiliac practice of causing partial suffocation to

enhance erotic pleasure, and is often said to be related to the observation that hanged men get "death erections" and even ejaculate as they die (although in practice this is probably more to do with sudden massive trauma to the spinal cord). So how do you spot a "gasper"?

a) He's male: The overwhelming majority of asphyxiophiliacs are male.

b) He or she is sporting a badge bearing the legend RACK: This stands for Risk Aware Consensual Kink, and is a subculture in extreme BDSM (bondage, domination and sado-masochist) circles.

c) He or she mentions the phrase *edgeplay*. This is BDSM talk for risky business.

d) He or she has a large collection of scarves, but never wears them to go out. Scarves are a favorite tool for erotic asphyxiation, hence the term *scarfing*.

e) He or she owns a gas mask. Unless your partner is a veteran, this is an unusual item to have around the house. Gas masks are popular in BDSM breath control play.

f) He or she is found dead in compromising circumstances. Autoerotic asphyxia is a dangerous business, especially since many asphyxiophiliacs prefer to practice on their own. An "erotic" level of asphyxiation may be very close to unconsciousness, and once the person passes out he may be unable to stop the asphyxiation. Famous people thought to have died in this way include rock singer Michael Hutchence and British MP Stephen Milligan. Between 250 and 1000 people a year die in this way in the US alone, almost all of them male. Corpses are often found in suggestive circumstances—naked, with semen, surrounded by pornography, sex toys, etc.